Asperger Syndrome
and Difficult Moments

Asperger Syndrome and Difficult Moments

Practical Solutions for Tantrums, Rage, and Meltdowns

Brenda Smith Myles
and
Jack Southwick

Second Edition
Revised and Expanded

Autism Asperger Publishing Co.
P.O. Box 23173
Shawnee Mission, Kansas 66283-0173
www.asperger.net

AAPC

© 1999, 2005 by Autism Asperger Publishing Co.
First printing 1999
Second printing 2002
Third printing 2004
Second Edition 2005
P.O. Box 23173
Shawnee Mission, Kansas 66283-0173
www.asperger.net

Publisher's Cataloging-in-Publication
(provided by Quality Books, Inc.)

Myles, Brenda Smith.
    Asperger syndrome and difficult moments : practical solutions for tantrums, rage, and meltdowns / Brenda Smith Myles and Jack Southwick. -- New rev. and expanded ed.
    p. cm.
    Includes bibliographical references and index.
    ISBN 1-931282-70-6
    Library of Congress Control Number: 2005920050

    1. Asperger's syndrome. 2. Anger in children. 3. Southwick, Jack. I. Title.

RC553.A88M973 2005   616.85'8832
                      QBI04-200534

This book was previously published under the title
Asperger Syndrome and Rage : Practical Solutions for a Difficult Moment

This book is designed in Minion, Helvetica Neuland Extended, and Ellington

Managing Editor: Kirsten McBride
Cover Design: Taku Hagiwara
Production Assistant: Ginny Biddulph

Printed in the United States of America

Dedicated to the children
at Camp Determination,
who were the
inspiration for this book.

Contents

An Overview of the Characteristics of Asperger Syndrome That May Impact Behavior

In 1944, Hans Asperger, an Austrian physician, described the unique characteristics of four children he had seen in his clinic. These children had a common profile, which Asperger defined in the context of (a) physical appearance and expressive characteristics, (b) intelligence, (c) behavior within a social group, and (d) drive and affect. Challenges in these areas hindered the children in effectively engaging in social interactions at an early age. Asperger noted that even though these children experienced social deficits, they were capable of original thoughts and experiences that could lead to exceptional achievements and eventual social acceptability.

Over time, Asperger made some changes in his original conceptualization of the children he studied. However, the essential clinical characteristics remained the same. Asperger's work was primarily dormant until Wing (1981) brought attention to this exceptionality. In her seminal paper, she discussed Asperger's work and further elaborated by providing 34 case studies that showed surprising similarities to Asperger's findings. Since then, a number of studies and anecdotes have described and defined characteristics that have come to be referred to as Asperger Syndrome. Many of the essential descriptors outlined by Asperger have remained the same, leading researchers and writers such as Frith (1991) and Wing (1981) to conclude that Asperger's characterizations have withstood the test of time.

Over the past decade, this neurological disorder has increasingly been recognized by professionals and parents, particularly since the addition of Asperger Syndrome (AS) in the *International Classification of Diseases and Related Health Problems* (World Health Organization, 1992) (see Table 1.1) and *Diagnostic and Statistical Manual – 4th Edition, Text Revision* (American Psychological Association, 2000) (see Table 1.2). According to these documents, to receive a diagnosis of AS, an individual must exhibit some atypical form of repetitive patterns of behavior, interests, and activities. These behaviors can include but are not limited to: (a) an encompassing preoccupation in one or more areas of interest, (b) an inflexible adherence to a nonfunctional routine or ritual, (c) repetitive motor movements, or (d) a persistent preoccupation with parts of objects.

The following provides a brief discussion of specific characteristics related to AS in the areas of (a) cognition, (b) language, (c) socialization, (d) sensory issues, (e) visual processing, and (f) behavior.

Cognition

Over 50 years ago, Asperger reported an adult-like intellectual functioning in the children he observed related to a limited number of special interests. That is, these children looked at things from a different viewpoint and thought about problems that were far beyond the perceived interests or the intellectual level of same-age peers.

Currently, researchers and practitioners recognize that although the vast majority of students with AS have average to above-average intellectual abilities and are included in general education classrooms, they experience academic problems. Indeed, social and communication deficits combined with obsessive and narrowly defined interests, concrete and literal thinking, inflexibility, poor problem-solving and organizational skills, difficulty in discerning relevant from irrelevant stimuli, and weak social standing often make it difficult for students with AS to fully benefit from unadapted general education curricula and instructional systems. As a result, a number of children and youth with AS are thought to have learning disabilities (Frith, 1991).

Children and youth with AS have a neurological disorder. Even though they have the same level of intelligence as other children, the neurological difference impacts how they think, feel, and react. Dunn, Myles, and Orr (2002) confirmed this finding. For example, in their investigation of sensory issues in AS, Dunn and colleagues found that many individuals with AS have

Table 1.1
Asperger Syndrome Definition:
International Classification of Diseases and Related Health Problems – Tenth Edition

A disorder of uncertain nosological validity, characterized by the same kind of qualitative abnormalities of reciprocal social interaction that typify autism, together with a restricted, stereotyped repetitive repertoire of interests and activities. The disorder differs from autism primarily in that there is no general delay or retardation in language or cognitive development. Most individuals are of normal general intelligence but it is common for them to be markedly clumsy; the condition occurs predominantly in boys (in a ratio of about eight boys to one girl). It seems highly likely that at least some cases represent mild varieties of autism, but it is uncertain whether or not that is so for all. There is a strong tendency for abnormalities to persist into adolescence and adult life and it seems that they represent individual characteristics that are not greatly affected by environmental influences. Psychotic episodes occasionally occur in early adult life.

Diagnostic Guidelines

Diagnosis is based on the combination of a lack of any clinically significant general delay in language or cognitive development plus, as with autism, the presence of qualitative deficiencies in restricted, repetitive, stereotyped patterns of behavior, interests, and activities.

There may or may not be problems in communication similar to those associated with autism, but significant language retardation would rule out the diagnosis.

Includes: autistic psychopathy

schizoid disorder of childhood

Excludes: anankastic personality disorder (F60.5)

attachment disorders of childhood (F94.1, F94.2)

obsessive-compulsive disorder (F21)

schizotypal disorder (F21)

simple schizophrenia (F20.6)

Table 1.2
Diagnostic Criteria for
Asperger's Disorder (299.80):
Diagnostic and Statistical Manual of Mental
Disorders – Fourth Edition, Text Revision

A. Qualitative impairment in social interaction, as manifested by at least two of the following:
  (1) marked impairment in the use of multiple nonverbal behaviors such as eye-to-eye gaze, facial expression, body postures, and gestures to regulate social interaction
  (2) failure to develop peer relationships appropriate to developmental level
  (3) a lack of spontaneous seeking to share enjoyment, interests, or achievements with other people (e.g., by a lack of showing, bringing, or pointing out objects of interest to other people)
  (4) lack of social or emotional reciprocity

B. Restricted repetitive and stereotyped patterns of behavior, interests, and activities, as manifested by at least one of the following:
  (1) encompassing preoccupation with one or more stereotyped and restricted patterns of interest that is abnormal either in intensity or focus
  (2) apparently inflexible adherence to specific, nonfunctional routines or rituals
  (3) stereotyped and repetitive motor mannerisms (e.g., hand or finger flapping or twisting, or complex whole-body movements)
  (4) persistent preoccupation with parts of objects

C. The disturbance causes clinically significant impairment in social, occupational, or other important areas of functioning.

D. There is no clinically significant delay in language (e.g., single words used by age 2 years, communicative phrases used by 3 years).

E. There is no clinically significant delay in cognitive development or in the development of age-appropriate self-help skills, adaptive behavior (other than in social interaction), and curiosity about the environment in childhood.

F. Criteria are not met for another specific Pervasive Developmental Disorder or Schizophrenia.

poor auditory processing and modulation (i.e., poor ability to regulate responses). Hence, when these children become stressed, they have limited ability to calm themselves or control their behavior. In addition, when children have poor modulation, their responses can vary dramatically from one situation to another, making it difficult to predict how they will behave in a given situation.

The result is that the child with AS may engage in rage behavior or blurt out inappropriate phrases because he has limited self-control under stress. It is important to note, however, that when not under stress, children and youth with AS think and feel as others do.

Generalization

A challenge facing children and youth with AS relates to their difficulty in generalizing knowledge and skills. That is, they frequently have problems applying information and skills across settings and with different individuals as well as integrating learned material and experience. While students may memorize sets of facts, these lists often remain unconnected bits of information. For example, such students may be able to cite a rule or set of procedures that they are to follow in a given situation, but be incapable of applying them when needed. Teachers often voice concern over this lack of generalization, misinterpreting the lack of symmetry between verbalization and actions as intentional misbehavior.

For example, Fred's typical strategy to engage others in play was to tell his peers what to do. Following even a minor lack of compliance on the part of playmates, Fred would swing at the peer closest to him. Fred's counselor worked with him on developing a strategy to help him cope better when playmates did not engage in an activity the way Fred wanted them to. Fred's strategy was to:

1. Suggest an activity.
2. If his peers indicated an unwillingness to play, he would ask them to play the game again.
3. If the playmates still did not want to engage in Fred's choice of activity, then he would either agree to play another game and suggest his game for next time or tell the peers good-bye and find other children with the same interests as his own. Fred verbalized this strategy from cue cards and role-played it in the counselor's office with repeated accuracy. However, when an actual situation occurred on the playground, Fred immediately revert-

ed back to his hitting strategy. The counselor, observing the scene, threw up his hands and said, "Fred must not want to play with the other boys. He knew what he was supposed to do. He just chose not to do it." However, the truth is that Fred was not willfully disobedient, he simply had not generalized the necessary skills beyond verbalization and cued role-play.

This situation is typical of many children with AS. One explanation for this phenomenon is their neurological immaturity. Two important abilities affect maturity: (a) the ability to retrieve learned behavior from the area of the brain in which it is "filed" for future reference; and (b) the ability to "read," "interpret," and "act" on social clues received from the environment. Both of these abilities are based on using the "thinking" part of the brain, which does not function well under stress in children with AS and other neurological disabilities. It is no wonder, then, that these children misinterpret social situations and, even with knowledge of how to "act", resort to practiced strategies that they have had in their repertoire for some time.

The analogy of the brain to a computer may help explain the process of how learned behavior is "filed" in the brain and retrieved for later use. When stress affects a child with a neurological disorder, the child is less able to access the "thinking" area of the brain. Therefore, the child does not act in what others perceive to be a logical or rational manner.

This tendency to retrieve established behavioral patterns under stressful circumstances also helps explain why a child may act a certain way even though she has learned better and more acceptable ways of handling a situation. That is, the child may be unable to retrieve a particular newly learned behavior when under stress, yet be capable of recalling it an hour later when not under stress. For example, the parent may say, "What were you thinking about! You knew better! We went over this just last week." And the child will respond, "I don't know – I guess I just was not thinking." (Translation: The child, under stress, did not retrieve the newest learned behavior; instead, previously well-practiced behavior was retrieved.)

Maturity

Maturity is often assessed by our actions in social situations. To be socially adept, people must be able to perceive and understand social clues such as frowns, smiles, boredom, emotions, etc. They must be able to think clearly about their own behavior and the behavior of others. They must make sound judgments about the persons around them. All these skills require thinking and, as mentioned, thinking is difficult for the child with neurological difficulties when under stress. As a result, children with these difficulties, such as children with AS, appear "clueless" or "naive." A rule of thumb: Children with neurological difficulties have an emotional maturity level that is significantly below their chronological age. That is, children with AS may appear to have the emotional maturity of someone two-thirds their age.

Rote Memory

Although rote memory may be perceived as an asset, it can be a great detriment for persons with AS. Because of well-developed rote memory skills, persons with AS often give the impression that they understand concepts when in fact they do not. Typically, the person with AS picks up from context or conversation certain words or phrases and uses them in a rote manner that mimics comprehension. Often this parroting gives the impression that the person has well-developed higher-level comprehension skills, whereas comprehension is often actually only at the factual level. That is, persons with AS can understand basic facts in written material and either repeat them verbatim or paraphrase them. For example, students may be able to repeat the steps to completing a long division problem, but be unable to perform it. Similarly, they may answer multiple-choice questions on a worksheet about a novel they have read, but be unable to understand the main character's motivation.

Rote memory may be a disadvantage for students with AS in another way. Educators assume that good rote memory means that students can remember, at any time, pieces of information or events. But this is not true for many persons with AS. While chunks of information are stored in memory, it is often difficult for persons with this exceptionality to determine how to retrieve them. Open-ended questions, such as "Tell me what the main character in the story did after his horse disappeared," may not trigger a response because the student has stored the information under the main character's name and is unable to make the transition from the term "main character" to her actual name.

In students with AS, therefore, an exceptional memory is not related to the ability to recall information. For example, a friend who has an adult son with AS met for dinner a young man who was traveling through town. This young man was recently admitted to MIT, a highly competitive university. My friend began polite conversation with the young man by asking him to tell a bit about himself. The MIT admittee made fleeting eye contact and informed my friend that he could not answer open-ended questions. This response came from a person who had passed entrance examinations into MIT – a person who obviously was able to finish high school with a high grade point average and complete MIT entrance examinations with a high skill level.

Theory of Mind Deficits

Persons with AS are seen to have as one of their core cognitive deficits difficulties with "theory of mind." Some think that it is this deficit that sets children with AS and autism apart from those with other disabilities (Baron-Cohen, Jolliffe, Mortimore, & Robertson, 1997; Blackshaw, Kinderman, Hare, & Hatton, 1991; Gillberg, 1993; Lawson, Baron-Cohen, & Wheelwright, 2004; Leslie, 1987). In brief, people with theory of mind problems have difficulty understanding the emotions and mental states of others. The concepts of systematizing and empathizing have been investigated within theory of mind. Lawson and others (2004) found that individuals with AS were more likely to experience challenges in empathizing – the drive to identify emotions in others and react to them appropriately – but to exhibit strengths in systematizing, such as understanding the workings of a machine, mathematics, and taxonomies.

As illustrated below, theory of mind problems have a profound impact on persons with AS. Those exhibiting difficulties in this area experience the following multitude of academic, behavior, and social problems.

1. Difficulty explaining own behaviors

Even though persons with AS are highly verbal, they have difficulty explaining why they did something. Even if they have a rationale for engaging in a behavior or social interaction, they often cannot give an adequate explanation.

2. Difficulty understanding emotions

Many students with AS understand a limited number of emotions. They may only recognize two to three emotions along the continuum from extremely happy to very sad. For example, when they get 100% on a weekly spelling test they are extremely happy, and they may exhibit the same degree of emotion when they receive a new bike. There is little understanding of subtleties. By comparison, the typical person may be pleased to receive 100% on the test, but be overjoyed to have a new bike.

Not only do persons with AS have difficulty recognizing the emotions of others, they often have problems understanding their own feelings. They may have difficulty understanding their own state of mind. They may be unable to recognize that they are agitated and that this agitation, unless addressed, may lead to behavior problems.

3. Difficulty predicting the behavior or emotional state of others

Many of our actions and reactions are dictated by how we think others will feel. In school, when a teacher says she is not feeling well, most students understand that the teacher may not be as patient as usual and that today is not a good day for practical jokes. Those with AS do not see this obvious connection between not feeling well and lack of patience. When they pull a practical joke, therefore, they are surprised by the teacher's negative response.

4. Problems understanding the perspectives of others

Teachers often give assignments that require students to assume the role of a historical character, involving writing papers or plays or making a speech impersonating the historical figure. Tasks of this nature are difficult for those who do not understand the human experience from different perspectives. Since persons with AS have difficulty understanding their own state of mind, they can hardly be expected to be able to imagine the state of mind of others.

5. Problems inferring the intentions of others

Every day, Jorge, a high school student with AS, walks into the school cafeteria where he is greeted by a group of typically achieving peers. His friends routinely ask, "What's up?" Each day, Jorge looks up to the ceiling to see what is up. The peers laugh. Jorge thinks these boys are his friends. In reality, they are not friends; they are making fun of Jorge.

6. Lack of understanding that behavior impacts how others think and/or feel

Many people with AS do not make the connection between their actions and others' reactions to them. Jonathan, a young boy with AS, really wanted to play with Bill on the playground. Jonathan could not understand the relationship between Jonathan's hitting Bill out of anger several times and Bill's unwillingness to associate with him.

7. Problems with joint attention and other social conventions

Persons with AS have difficulties with turn-taking, perspective-taking, politeness, and numerous other social conventions. Mary, whose passion was earthquakes, would walk up to people and begin to spout facts about the latest earthquakes around the world. Further, if someone else attempted to speak with her, she would reply with earthquake statistics. She did not perceive her behavior as problematic and a reason why people would turn away.

John was perceived by many of his peers as crazy. His conversation would change course, sometimes in mid-sentence. For example, his first sentence would be about a basketball game score ("Forty-six to 44. Could you believe it?") without reference to team names or even a statement that he was discussing a game. His second sentence would begin with a phrase about the material his t-shirt was made of. In the middle of this sentence, he would make a seemingly random statement about the great taste of jello. He did not understand that the listener could not follow his conversation. To John, it made sense. He was interested in a basketball game he had seen the previous evening, his t-shirt felt "scratchy," and he wanted jello for lunch.

8. Problems differentiating fiction from fact

A young man has spent a significant amount of time drawing plans and writing technical reports on how to improve the capability of the Star Trek Enterprise. He sees this vehicle as actually existing, and his passion regarding some of the architectural components that he has introduced is often convincing to others who spend time with him. Everyone else knows that the Enterprise is fictional and does not understand the student's inability to understand that it is not reality (Cumine, Leach, & Stevenson, 1998; Jordan & Powell, 1995).

Problem-Solving

While students may be able to engage in high-level thinking and problem-solving when their area of interest is involved, these skills are often not used throughout the school day. Many students with AS select one problem-solving strategy and use it consistently regardless of the situation or outcome. For example, if the school locker does not open, the student may keep trying the same combination over and over. Although this strategy can be effective, when repeated attempts prove unsuccessful, there needs to be a self-monitoring component.

That is, if the student has tried the correct locker combination five times unsuccessfully, chances are that there is another problem with the locker. However, students with AS might not know the problem-solving strategy that involves asking an adult or peer when difficulty arises and that alternate options are necessary. As a result, persistence, if unsuccessful, can result in inappropriate behavioral outbursts.

Difficulty accessing information or strategies may make problem-solving even more difficult. Although the student may be able to recite several problem-solving strategies and realize that they can be generalized, she may not be able to recall any of these strategies when they are needed. Because the student with AS often has difficulty searching her memory for particular facts, she may not be able to access that given strategy. Thus, even if the student has an effective system for retrieving problem-solving strategies, it is still likely that she cannot use this system. By the time the student cognitively realizes that a problem exists, she typically is so confused, angry, or disoriented that her reaction is behavioral – a tantrum or withdrawal.

Problem-solving becomes even more difficult in academics if abstract concepts are involved. Thus, persons with AS frequently have difficulty with word problems, estimation, algebra, and geometry, all of which require problem-solving skills and often contain a high level of abstraction.

The deficits of some students with AS are not easily recognized. Their pedantic style, advanced vocabulary, and grammatically perfect responses often mask their skill levels. Students with this exceptionality often fail to understand what they read despite average to above-average word-calling skills. Teachers, in turn, fail to recognize the special academic needs of students with AS because these children sound as if they understand more than they do. Students' inability to monitor their own skills also contributes to this problem. As one teacher reported, "Johnny reads much better than my other second graders and can answer many factual questions. It is as if he has memorized key words and phrases and can say them when he is cued. But, he often does this without having an overall understanding of what he has read." Another teacher stated, "Margaret has exceptional rote memory. She reads something once and recalls it verbatim. However, she doesn't know which information to memorize. Margaret memorized the entire list of food and nonfood items brought aboard the Mayflower by the Pilgrims, but did not understand why they had undertaken their journey to America."

Language

Frith (1991) observed that children with AS "tend to speak fluently by the time they are five, even if their language development was slow to begin with, and even if their language is noticeably odd in its use for communication" (p. 3). Asperger described language onset for children with AS as occurring at the expected age, while others reported that many children with AS are slow to talk. Many individuals diagnosed with AS reveal a variety of communication deficits as infants, and many of their perceived "special abilities" may be explained as rote responses rather than normal or precocious language development. According to the DSM-IV, TR (APA, 2000), in order to be diagnosed with AS, a child must have no significant delay in language.

Many children and youth with AS have good structural language skills, such as clear pronunciation and correct syntax, but poor pragmatic communication abilities. Thus, many use poor language for social interaction and interactive communication. For example, a child may (a) repeat the same phrase over and over, (b) talk with exaggerated inflections or in a monotone and droning style, (c) discuss at length a single topic that is of little interest to others, or (d) experience difficulty in sustaining conversation unless it focuses exclusively on a particular narrowly defined topic. These communication problems are not surprising, given that effective communication requires that individuals have mutually shared topics to communicate about and are willing to listen as well as to talk – common problems for persons with AS. Moreover, the adult-like and pedantic speaking style of some children and youth with AS may further lessen their appeal to their peers.

As previously stated, nonverbal communication deficits and related social context communication problems are common among persons with AS. This includes problems relating to (a) proxemics, or standing closer to or farther away from another person during conversation than is customarily accepted; (b) intensely staring at another person for long periods while interacting; (c) maintaining abnormal body posture in social situations; (d) failing to make eye contact or displaying an inexpressive face, thereby failing to signal interest, approval or disapproval of another person during conversation; and (e) failing to use or understand gestures and facial expressions that accompany verbal messages.

Related to school-based interactions, students with AS frequently experience difficulty in comprehending language related to describing abstract concepts; understanding and correctly using figures of speech such as metaphors, idioms, parables, and allegories; and grasping the meaning and intent of rhetorical questions. A story with a moral of "Don't cry over spilled milk" might be confusing for a student with AS. She might look for a milk-spilling incident in the story or draw a conclusion that the moral literally means that when milk is spilled, it should just be cleaned up, and people should not cry. Since these conventions are commonly used by authors of school texts and classroom teachers, deficits in this area have a negative impact on the academic success of students with AS.

Visual Processing

Related to the area of language is visual processing. Although it has been well documented that children and youth with autism process visual information better than auditory information (Quill, 1995), the same type of data does not exist on individuals with AS. Despite this dearth of evidence, practitioners generally agree that visually presented information is more easily understood by individuals with this exceptionality. Thus, to best understand their environment, students with AS need visual supports.

Socialization

Social relationships in the children Asperger described were a source of conflict early in life. In fact, he reported that one of the hallmark characteristics of these children was an inability to build and maintain social relationships. Asperger posited that the children he studied were often socially isolated because of their seeming lack of interest in what was going on around them, their engagement in stereotypic behaviors, and their tendency to follow their own impulses and interests regardless of others' responses. He also noted that if another individual intruded on the world of a person with this exceptionality, it might prompt an aggressive reaction.

Reciprocal social interaction problems found in AS are numerous. The inability to interact with peers is marked by (a) lack of understanding of social cues, (b) a tendency to interpret words and/or phrases concretely, and (c) language comprehension problems. In addition, persons with AS often exhibit a clumsy social style, engage in one-sided social interactions, and have difficulty accurately sensing the feelings of others or taking others' perspective. These children either monopolize or have little to no participation in conversation, show abnormalities in inflection, and repeat phrases inappropriately and out of context.

The social rules considered second nature by many are not innately understood by many persons with AS. One theory suggests that the impairment in two-way social interaction arises from a lack of ability to understand and use the rules governing social behavior. Individuals with AS do not know how to initiate and/or maintain a conversation, monitor others' interest in what is being said, use polite verbal and nonverbal cues, or understand such cues given by others. The idea that people may not say what they mean in conversation is also foreign to them. "Go jump in the lake" may mean to a person with AS that she is to find a body of water and immerse herself in it. Further, the young man with this exceptionality who is asked "How are you?" may give a lengthy and detailed response about his physical and emotional condition, thinking that the person who asked the question actually is interested in an honest response.

Individuals with AS are often seen engaging in simple, routine social interactions such as greetings. However, many are not able to extend this interaction in a meaningful way. When they do attempt to maintain a conversation, it is often marked by language considered inappropriate. It is as if the filter between the brain and the mouth is not cooperating – they say exactly what comes to mind. This is often called "blurting." "That red dress makes you look fat" or "What you said is stupid" may be uttered by somebody with AS. There is no intention to hurt or make fun; the person is merely stating something as he sees it. Because of incidents like these, people with AS are commonly described as lacking an awareness of accepted social protocol and common sense, displaying a propensity to misinterpret social cues and unspoken messages, and being inclined to display a variety of socially unaccepted and non-reciprocal responses.

To many persons with AS, conversation exists primarily as a means of talking about a topic that is fascinating to them, regardless of audience input or interest. Without the ability to monitor others' thoughts or value the input of others, they often engage in extensive monologues on a restricted topic. They do not understand that when a person rolls her eyes, crosses her arms, or backs away she is signaling a lack of interest in what is being said.

In spite of their frequent lack of social awareness, many individuals with AS are aware that they are different from their peers. Thus, self-esteem problems, self-fault finding, and self-deprecation are common among individuals with AS. These problems are exacerbated when the child feels that he cannot control his behavior.

For some of these reasons, children and youth with AS are poor incidental social learners. That is, many learn social skills without fully understanding their meaning and context. Sometimes they attempt to rigidly and broadly follow universal social rules, because doing so provides structure to an otherwise confusing world. Unfortunately, this is often not a successful strategy because there are few, if any, universal and inflexible social rules. For example, most middle school students curse. Despite being unable to learn appropriate social skills incidentally, Margery has learned from peers some particularly colorful curse words. She has observed children cursing on the school soccer field and applies the universal rule that cursing is okay outside. She does not, however, learn the nuance that you should not curse when the principal is standing beside you. Consequently, she is thrown into a state of confusion when the principal threatens to punish her for what she considers to be a socially appropriate behavior. Another student, Scott, learns from a peer that it is okay to whisper to peers during seatwork in Mrs. Thompson's class. All students in this class are allowed to ask each other for help and visit as long as it does not hinder assignment completion. But Scott is sent to the office after applying this universal rule in Ms. Swanson's class where the unstated rule and expectation is that no talking is allowed during seatwork. Scott does not understand that different expectations may exist in different settings and that his behavior must change accordingly.

Sensory Issues

Asperger reported that the children and youth he observed were prone to peculiar sensory stimuli responses. For example, children with AS are often hypersensitive to certain sounds or visual stimuli, such as fluorescent lights, and may respond negatively when overloaded with these types of sensory stimuli. Parents and teachers have reported behavior problems associated with these children's fear of anticipated unpleasant sensory stimuli such as city whistle signals, chimes, or fire alarms that are sounded at certain times. Additionally, it is common for parents of children with AS to report that these children have a strong and obsessive preference for certain foods and textures (e.g., child will only wear clothes made of certain fabrics or cannot tolerate clothing tags touching skin); and some individuals with AS have been found to have an extremely high tolerance for physical pain. Other parents of children with AS have related problems with their children getting their socks to fit "just right" so that the toe seam does not rub their feet.

Reports on sensory problems for persons with AS are largely anecdotal. However, a preliminary descriptive study appears to support parent observations and the contentions of persons with AS themselves. Dunn et al.

(2002) found that parents and educators of children and youth with AS frequently observed the following sensory behaviors in their children and students: (a) are distracted or have trouble focusing in the presence of varied stimuli; (b) prefer quiet, sedentary games; (c) have difficulty paying attention; (d) prefer certain tastes; (e) have difficulty tolerating changes in plans and expectations; (f) exhibit low frustration tolerance; and (g) seem anxious. Similarly, in the norming of a survey to identify children as having AS, sensory items on the checklist failed to differentiate children with AS from those with autism. That is, both groups displayed a similar profile (Myles, Simpson, & Bock, 1999).

Behavior

While behavioral problems are not universal among students with AS, they are not uncommon. When behavioral difficulties do occur, they typically appear to be a function of (a) social ineptness, (b) lack of understanding, (c) a high stress level, (d) lack of control over the environment, (e) an obsessive and single-minded pursuit of a certain interest, or (f) a defensive panic reaction. The behavior problems of children with AS are connected to their more generalized inability to function in a world they perceive as unpredictable and threatening. Thus, there appears to be little support for Asperger's original description of children with AS as malicious and mean-spirited.

On the behavioral continuum, children and youth with AS may range from withdrawn to active. Regardless of where they fall on this continuum, however, they are routinely viewed as socially awkward and stiff, emotionally blunted, self-centered, unable to understand nonverbal social cues, inflexible, and lacking in empathy and understanding. Therefore, even when children and adolescents with AS actively seek out others, they usually encounter social isolation because of their lack of understanding of the rules of social behavior, including eye contact, proximity to others, gestures, posture, and so forth.

Stress and Excitement

It is also common for individuals with AS to become emotionally vulnerable and easily stressed. In fact, some argue that persons with AS are under constant or near-constant stress. Wanting to play with another child and not knowing how, trying to follow teacher directions but not understanding what is being said, hearing children laugh around you and not getting the joke – these are all stressful situations that children and youth with AS experience daily.

Thus, many individuals with AS experience severe social anxiety (Barnhill et al., 2000; Bellini, 2004) that impacts every facet of their lives, including their behavior. Sometimes children and youth with AS appear to be over-controlling – attempting to control the day's schedule or people around them. Individuals who see themselves as having less control over their environment and their lives are more anxious, so their controlling behavior may actually lessen their stress and anxiety (Bellini, 2004).

Research has shown that children and youth with AS often misinterpret the actions of others as aggressive (Carothers & Taylor, 2004; Kaland et al., 2002). For example, adolescents tend to misinterpret a resting face or casual facial expression as being aggressive. Maura, a 14-year-old with AS, was accused of being aggressive toward a teacher and peer. Both said that Maura hit them without provocation. When Maura was able to explain what happened, she said that she thought her teacher and peer looked as if they were going to hurt her. Children with AS may become agitated by something as simple as perceiving others as invading their private space in the lunch line or when they find themselves in the midst of several simultaneous social activities. However, unlike many typically developing and achieving peers, many children with AS do not reveal their stress through voice tone, body posture, and so forth. As a result, their agitation often escalates to a point of crisis because of others' unawareness of their discomfort, along with their own inability to monitor and control uncomfortable situations. Further, their behaviors are often exacerbated by fatigue.

Excitement often causes the same reaction as stress. Many parents report that they cannot tell their child with AS in advance of a highly favored activity. The child, in anticipation, becomes overexcited, cannot monitor his behavior, and loses control. Many households have forbidden their children to "horse around," that age-old game where children playfully touch each other and wrestle. Children with AS often become too engrossed in horse play and cannot control their level of interaction with a peer.

Given these deficits, it is not surprising that children and youth with AS are relatively easy targets for peers prone to teasing and bullying. One young man with AS, Mark, was almost always near crisis. Rigid in how he thought other high school students should behave, he carried around the school code of conduct and when he saw an infraction (e.g., someone cursing), he would approach the offending party and recite the rule that was being broken and even the page number where the offense appeared in the manual. Many students did not appreciate Mark's law-abiding behavior. One day when several boys were smoking outside of school in front of Mark, he became extremely anxious, citing that the school did not allow smoking. The students told Mark that the code book he had was out-of-date and that a new one had been printed that did allow smoking. Mark became even more anxious in his attempt to explain that his manual was current. Unable to convince the students that they were not supposed to smoke, he reverted to screaming.

Distractibility and Inattention

Many persons with AS have an attention deficit/hyperactivity disorder (ADHD) diagnosis at one time in their lives (Goldstein & Schwebach, 2004). Indeed, AS and ADHD share many commonalities, particularly in terms of distractibility and inattentiveness. Attention often seems fleeting. One moment, the student with AS may appear to be attending, the next moment he suddenly seems to withdraw into an inner world and be totally unaware of the environment. Teacher directions are not processed; student conversations are not heard. This daydreaming may occur over extended time periods, with no predictability. The daydreaming is often so intense that a physical prompt from the teacher is needed to call the student back to task. Often the antecedent is unknown, but it may be related to stress, focus on an obsessive interest, or overstimulation.

Even while attending, the student may not react to teacher instructions. For example, the student may start to follow a three-step direction, but appear to lose focus as she completes the first step. Rather than looking for a model or asking for help, she will look for a way out. The student may remain frozen in the same place, wander aimlessly about, shuffle through her desk, stare into space, or begin to daydream. On rare occasions, the student may cause a distraction or act out. Often these same behaviors are evidenced when the student is required to engage in nonpreferred work tasks for extended periods.

Social interactions are often distracting for persons with AS. Because they want to interact with others, they tend to focus all their attention on others in the classroom instead of on the tasks at hand. If the student has a particularly strong need to interact with a specific classmate, he may attend to that person exclusively, staring nonstop at the targeted individual or listening in on that person's conversations. If the person with AS and his classmate have developed a reciprocal relationship, the person with AS might unilaterally seek that person's approval before beginning a task or addressing the teacher or another student. This gives the peer an enormous amount of power over the person with AS. For example, the peer may prompt the student with AS to complete assignments for her, ask the student to break classroom rules, or prompt the student to engage in activities that will place him in jeopardy.

Distractions may also occur because students with AS do not know how to determine relevant from irrelevant stimuli. For example, the student with AS may focus on a particular picture or map in a textbook while other students in the class have moved on to the next chapter, or she may focus on the way a speaker's earring dangles when she moves her head instead of listening to the content of her lecture. At this time, the student may seem to have a "laser-like" focus on a particular object. A high level of frustration may occur when the student with AS attempts to memorize every fact associated with a particular World War II battle mentioned in the text, including an extensive list of weaponry. The student does not innately know that memorizing such information is not necessary.

Tunnel Vision

School requires that students attend to certain stimuli while screening out irrelevant, yet competing distractors. That is, at any given time a student might be expected to attend to a textbook and ignore (a) students talking around her, (b) a teacher offering another student help, and (c) a bulletin board that overviews a favored topic. This is often difficult for the student with AS for several reasons.

Tunnel vision impairs the student's ability to discern relevant from irrelevant information. If the bulletin board contains information on a topic of high interest, the student may consider it more important than a text. If a student with AS has a strong social attachment to someone across the room, interacting with that person might take precedence over any task the teacher assigned. Rational explanations that talking across the room is inappropriate may not impact the student with AS, who might seem "driven" to interact with his friend.

Tunnel vision also impacts logical thinking and flexibility. Students with AS logically group items or characteristics so that they can make sense of them. That is, they form a schema that is exact and often inflexible. For example, a student who learns the spelling rule, "I before E except after C," might apply the rule rigidly. The student would then be convinced that words like *neighbor* and *weigh* should be spelled *nieghbor* and *wiegh*, respectively.

Problems can present themselves when the student is reading for information, such as reading from a social studies text to answer questions on a worksheet. Generally, reading for information is difficult. Students with AS most likely will read to find specific text information presented on a worksheet or study guide and ignore and not process in a meaningful way information that they were not responsible for knowing. When the student is later tested and given questions that were not on the study guide, the student most likely will not answer those questions or answer them incorrectly, even if the information seems obvious to others.

Obsessions are another hallmark of tunnel vision. Two types of obsessions are generally exhibited by persons with AS. In the first type of obsession (primary), the student's level of interest is all-encompassing. As a result, a discussion of the topic of interest can escalate to almost tantrum-like behavior, where the student cannot control his discussion of the topic and behavior. Rapid speech, increased volume, a high-pitched voice, pacing, and hand wringing often occur with primary obsessions. Primary obsessions typically do not lend themselves to rational discussions and explorations (Myles & Simpson, 1998). That is, students cannot be talked out of them.

Secondary obsessions, on the other hand, refer to marked student interests wherein the student remains lucid, focused, and ready to learn about a particular topic. Students actively seek new information about the topic, but can be somewhat easily redirected. Often secondary interests are used by teachers to motivate students to complete academic tasks. Temple Grandin (2004), an adult with AS, suggests that secondary interests may be developed into career choices.

Structure, Organization, and Flexibility

Students with AS typically fall at the ends of the continuum of structure: they either have an inherent ability to provide structure or they totally rely on others to help them organize themselves. As a result, it is often said that students with AS have either the neatest or the messiest desks in class.

Nevertheless, it is generally easier for persons with AS to function in an organized environment. Predictable schedules, uniform assignment formats, and consistent teacher affect help these students devote their time and energy to academic tasks. Those who have internal structure tend to hold rigid expectations that schedules be followed and commitments be honored without fail. As a result, unscheduled events cause these student great dis-comfort, which can be manifested as disorientation, refusal to engage in the new activity, extended discourse about the canceled or postponed event, or behavior problems. In other words, the student communicates through lan-guage and behavior that change is difficult.

Educators comment that they have seen a student with AS tolerate change in some instances, but have evidenced other situations when the student lost control when the environment was altered. Sometimes students with AS can tolerate change, if that change occurs in only one dimension. For example, if library time is changed the student may adjust to the new schedule. However, if library time and the librarian change simultaneously, the same student may have difficulty maintaining any type of self-control.

Most students with AS have a limited ability to structure their own envi-ronment. A messy person with AS probably has not made a conscious choice to be that way; rather, he lacks good organizational skills. The student with this disability can literally lose a paper received only one minute earlier. He never has a pencil in class. The note that the teacher placed in the student's backpack never makes it home. Written work is not placed in a uniform manner on a page. The middle school student's locker is a mess; often he cannot locate his locker combination and when he does, he cannot find what he needs to get in his locker. He cannot organize his day by bringing both his science and his math book to science class even though his math class fol-lows immediately afterwards in the room next door. Almost every facet of the student's life is in disarray.

Teachers and parents often wonder how the student with AS gets from one place to another. It is a challenge to organize this type of student. Merely pro-viding a schedule or list of supplies is not enough. These aids are most often lost, so teachers must (a) help students learn organizational skills, (b) minimize loss of visual supports by velcroing them inside books or lockers, and (c) have additional copies of visual supports on hand when the student needs them.

Summary

The challenges and assets associated with AS are many and varied. The areas of (a) cognition, (b) language, (c) socialization, (d) sensory issues, (e) visual processing, and (f) behavior each presents with symptoms that differ-entiate these individuals from typically achieving children. Sometimes when the environment is structured in such a way that persons with AS can't have their needs met or don't understand behavioral, social, or academic expectations, an unfortunate event will occur – a rage attack, behavioral outburst or tantrum. Regardless of what name it is known by, such a reaction is debilitating to the person with AS and those around her. The following chapter discusses the phenomenon known as the rage cycle.

Throughout this book, we use the terms *rage*, *meltdowns*, and *tantrums* interchangeably to describe behavioral outbursts. Please note that these terms may also describe intense behaviors that may be internalized. Some children and youth turn these extreme behaviors inward.

CHAPTER 2

Tantrums, Rage, and Meltdowns

Anger – The False Façade

Act One, Scene Two (stage right)
Anger – The False Façade
Discover the real reason they might,
If only I would let down my guard.

Act Two, Scene Three (stage left)
Control – The Self-Power I Lack
My individuality now a case of theft,
Trust in the world I want back.

Act Three, Scene Four (center stage)
Fear – The True Feeling
Distractions and change inspire my rage,
My thoughts, my life are reeling.

Anger, Control, Fear
Backstage the applause I barely hear.
Look behind the set, beyond the curtains,
The scaffolds of emotions are becoming clear.

– Josie Santomauro*

*Josie is a writer and mother of a son with asperger syndrome. Josie's books include *Space Travelers, An Interactive Program for Developing Social Understanding, Social Competence and Social Skills for Students with Asperger Syndrome, Autism and Other Social Cognitive Challenges* (Shawnee Mission, KS: Autism Asperger Publishing Company, 2004).

Many students with Asperger Syndrome (AS) view school as a stressful environment that presents numerous stressors that are ongoing and of great magnitude. Common stressors include difficulty predicting events because of changing schedules, tuning in to and understanding teacher directions, interacting with peers, and anticipating differences in the environment such as classroom lighting, sounds/noises, odors, and so on.

Students with AS rarely indicate in ways that are meaningful to others that they are under stress or experiencing difficulty coping. In fact, they do not always know that they are near a stage of crisis themselves. Quite often they just "tune out" or daydream, or state in a monotone voice a seemingly benign phrase, such as "I don't know what to do." Since no emotion is conveyed, these behaviors often go unnoticed by adults. Then at a later point in time, the child engages, seemingly without provocation, in a verbally or physically aggressive event, often called a tantrum, rage, or meltdown. The child may begin to scream, kick over a desk, or totally shut down. There seems to be no predictability to this behavior; it just occurs.

Other students with AS do not display these types of behaviors in school. Sometimes teachers report that the student with AS is doing fine or managing in school in spite of academic and social problems. However, parents report that when their child arrives home, she loses control. That is, the child experiences a tantrum, rage, or meltdown at home. It seems as if some students use all their self-control to manage at school, and once they get to a safe environment (i.e., home), they let go of some of the pressure that is bottled up within them. Thus, regardless of where the stressor was encountered, the resulting meltdown can occur either at home or at school.

Although it may seem that way, meltdowns do not occur without warning! Rather, students with AS exhibit a pattern of behaviors that are precursors to a behavioral outburst. Sometimes these behaviors are subtle. In fact, those who do not know the student often report that a meltdown comes out of nowhere. One teacher reported, "Susan was just sitting at her desk quietly. The next thing I know she had a meltdown. She totally lost control, overturned her desk and began flailing her arms. I had no warning."

Without a clear understanding of rage and the cycle in which it occurs, it may indeed appear as if rage occurs without warning. This chapter explains the rage cycle and how it affects both children and the adults who work or live with them. For each stage, behaviors and interventions are outlined, including the importance of recognizing countercontrol and using teachable moments.

The Rage Cycle

Because tantrums, rage, and meltdowns occur for a reason, it is important to understand the underlying causes or antecedents that serve as triggers. The cycle typically runs through three stages: the rumbling stage, the rage stage, and the recovery stage (adapted from Albert, 1989; Beck, 1985). These stages can be of variable length, with one stage lasting hours and another only a few minutes.

The three stages can be conceptualized using a normal curve as illustrated in Figure 2.1 (Buron, personal communication, 2003; LaCava, personal communication, 2003). In fact, as shown, we are actually dealing with double curves. The outside curve illustrates the cycle the child progresses through when having a meltdown, whereas the inside curve depicts the cycle experienced by the adult who is with the child. Most people focus on the cycle experienced by the child, and rightfully so. However, understanding the stress experienced by the adult who is with the child is also important as such understanding can help us react better to children and youth with AS in the rage cycle.

Please note the teachable moments at each end of the curve. These are the ONLY times that the child is available to learn new skills. That is, when she is in the rumbling, rage or recovery stage, she cannot learn new skills and can only utilize skills that she already knows and is able to use fluently. This is important to recognize and respect. Failure to do so may escalate and prolong the cycle and will also cause frustration for the adult.

In the following, we will look at each of the three stages and present interventions that have been found to be effective for each.

Rumbling Stage

During the rumbling stage, students with AS exhibit specific behavioral changes that may not appear to be directly related to a meltdown. Students may bite their nails or lips, lower their voices, tense their muscles, tap their foot, grimace, or otherwise indicate general discontent. Students may also complain of not feeling well. It is easy to ignore these seemingly minor behaviors; yet, they often signal an impending crisis.

Some students engage in behaviors that are more pronounced, including withdrawing from others, either emotionally or physically, or lashing out at, or threatening the teacher or other students, either verbally or physically. The student may also challenge the classroom structure or authority by attempting to engage in a power struggle (see Table 2.1).

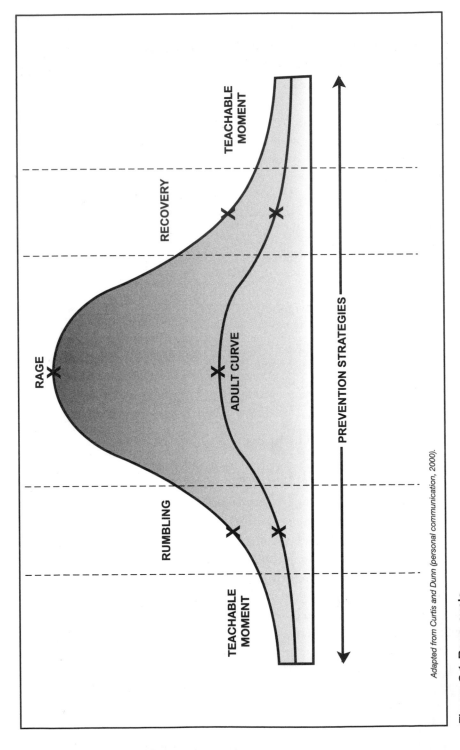

Adapted from Curtis and Dunn (personal communication, 2000).

Figure 2.1. Rage cycle.

Table 2.1
Typical Rumbling Stage Behaviors by Children and Youth

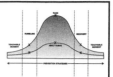

- Fidgeting
- Swearing
- Making noises
- Ripping paper
- Grimacing
- Refusing to cooperate
- Rapid movements

- Tears
- Tensing muscles
- Name calling
- Increasing/decreasing voice volume
- Verbal threats
- Tapping foot

It is important to observe and analyze a child's behavior and the environment when she experiences tantrums and rage, as well as track changes at home, school, and the community. This is discussed further in Chapter 3.

Child Behavior During the Rumbling Stage

During this stage, it is imperative that the teacher intervene with the student without becoming part of a struggle. The emphasis here is on teacher intervention because research has shown many students with AS do not recognize that they are under stress or are experiencing discomfort associated with the rumbling state (Barnhill et al., 2000). During this stage, effective teacher interventions often fall under the realm of surface behavior management (Long, Morse, & Newman, 1976). That is, teachers can use a variety of strategies such as antiseptic bouncing, proximity control, signal interference, or touch control to stop future behavior problems. Each of these strategies (see Table 2.2) will be briefly discussed in the following.

Table 2.2
Rumbling Stage Interventions

- Antiseptic bouncing
- Proximity control
- Signal interference
- Touch control
- Defusing tension through humor
- Support from routine

- Interest boosting
- Redirecting
- Cool zone
- Acknowledging student difficulties
- Just walk and don't talk

Antiseptic Bouncing

Antiseptic bouncing involves removing a student, in a nonpunitive fashion, from the environment in which she is experiencing difficulty. For example, Keisha is asked to take a note to the teacher across the hall. Jerome is asked to go to the art area to clean up supplies. Andy, who is asked to deliver the lunch count to the office, typically does not go directly from his classroom to the office. Rather, he stops by the water fountain, wanders by the classroom of a friend, stops to say hello to the custodian, and then gets to the office. His way back to the classroom is equally circuitous. During this time, Jerome has had an opportunity to regain a sense of calm. When he returns to the class, the problem has typically diminished in magnitude, and the teacher is on hand for support if needed.

Proximity Control

Rather than calling attention to a child's behavior, using this strategy the teacher moves near the student who is engaged in the behavior. Often something as simple as standing next to a student is calming and can be easily accomplished without interrupting the lesson. The teacher who circulates through the classroom during a lesson is using proximity control.

Signal Interference

Using signal interference, when the student begins to exhibit a seemingly minor precursor behavior, such as tapping his foot, the teacher gives a nonverbal signal to let the student know that she is aware of the situation. For example, the teacher may place herself in a position from which she can maintain eye contact with the student. Or a "secret "signal between teacher and the student can be used as a cue to watch the problem behavior. Many teachers snap their fingers, flick a light switch, or look away to indicate that inappropriate behavior is occurring. These techniques can be used to prevent more severe behaviors from occurring.

Touch Control

Sometimes a simple touch can serve to stop behavior. Gently touching the foot or leg of a student who is tapping his feet loudly may stop disruptive behavior.

Defusing Tension Through Humor

This technique involves using a joke or humorous remark in a potentially tense or potentially eruptive moment. A joke can often prevent group contagion from occurring and salvage an interrupted lesson. When using this approach, care must be taken to ensure that the student understands the humor and does not perceive himself as the target of a joke. In addition, it appears that some adults are better at using this technique than others. Adults who are not "gifted" with this ability should not make this their first intervention choice during the rumbling stage as misunderstood humor can escalate to the rage stage.

Support From Routine

Displaying a chart or visual schedule of class expectations and events of the day can provide a sense of security, which is important to many students with AS. The same technique can also be used as advance preparation for a change in routine. Informing students of schedule changes can prevent anxiety and save the teacher and class from disruption. For example, the student who is signaling frustration by snapping his fingers may be directed to his schedule to make him aware that after he completes two more problems, he gets to work on a topic of special interest with a peer.

Interest Boosting

Sometimes showing a personal interest in a student and her hobbies can encourage her. This involves (a) making the student aware that you recognize her individual preferences or (b) structuring lessons around a topic of interest. Interest boosting can often stop or prevent off-task or acting-out behavior.

Summary

The strategies presented above can be effective in stopping the rage cycle. They are particularly invaluable in that they can help the student regain control without stopping the class routine or calling undue attention to the student with AS. Intervention at this point is important so that the child retains her respect and dignity.

Strategies that do not fall under the category of surface management may also be used during the rumbling stage. They are similar to surface management strategies in that they are therapeutic, nonpunitive, and designed to support student success. These include redirecting, cool zone, acknowledging student difficulties, and "just walk and don't talk."

Redirecting

Redirecting involves helping the student to focus on something other than the task at hand. When the source of the behavior is a lack of understanding, telling the student that he and you can cartoon the situation in order to figure out what to do often works well for students with AS. Sometimes the student can "pull it together" until cartooning (see Chapter 4) can be done at a later time; at other times, the student may need to cartoon immediately. Redirection to a special interest topic or to an intervention suggested by an occupational therapist can also be effective.

Cool Zone

Ethan and Amanda Lautenschlager (personal communication, 2004) created the term "cool zone" (which is synonymous to "home base") to describe a place where students can go when they feel a need to regain control. Resource rooms or counselors' offices can serve as cool zones. One student uses the custodian's office as his cool zone. When students feel the need to leave the classroom, they can take assignments to the cool zone and work on them there in a less stressful environment. For some students it is helpful to schedule their days so that they begin at the cool zone with frequent stops throughout the day in the classroom with a teacher they have rapport with. In this way, students have a teacher with whom they have a consistent and positive relationship as well as a place to retreat to when the need arises (Myles & Simpson, 1998). Going to the cool zone can stop the child from progressing to the rage stage.

Acknowledging Student Difficulties

When the student is in the midst of the rumbling stage, it is sometimes effective for the teacher to state the rule to which the student should adhere universally and back it up through personalization and proximity. That is, the teacher should clearly state the rule along with the student's name, indicating that "everyone in the class follows the rule." Although face-to-face contact is not recommended, close proximity when communicating a rule and direct eye contact intensify the power of the message.

Under no circumstances should the teacher engage in lengthy conversation about "who is right" or "who is in control" (Valentine, 1987). This will only encourage escalation of the target behavior. For example, when working on a math problem the student begins to say, "This is too hard." The teacher, knowing the student can complete the problem, refocuses the student's attention by saying, "Yes, the problem is difficult. Let's do number one together." Often, just such an acknowledgment and a brief direction prevents the student from getting stuck in the rumbling stage. The teacher who uses this strategy must understand the child well enough to know that the child can hold himself together to do the problem. However, it should be noted that this strategy is effective only if the behavior or skill is a confirmed part of the student's repertoire. In other words, it should not be used when new or emerging skills or behaviors are involved.

In another situation, the teacher might say, "McKenzie, when it is difficult to finish work, we use the cool zone to help students stay on track. Please take your work to the cool zone." He may then place an icon that says "cool zone" on McKenzie's desk. In yet another scenario, the teacher might state, "You can play with the ball until the timer sounds, then it is Marvin's turn. In this class, we all take turns." At this critical juncture, the teacher might want to reinforce his verbalizations with an icon. The teacher uses a calm, but firm voice and avoids moving in a manner that could seem threatening.

Just Walk and Don't Talk

Sometimes an effective strategy is to walk with the student, unless the student is a "runner." The adult should walk with the student without talking because during the rumbling stage, anything the adult says is usually the wrong thing. The child is not thinking logically and will most likely react emotively to any adult statement, misinterpreting it or rephrasing it in such a way that its original intent is not recognizable. On this walk the child can say whatever she wishes without fear of disciplining or logical argument. The adult should be calm, show as little reaction as possible, and never be confrontational.

Summary

When selecting a technique for use during the rumbling stage, it is important to know the student, as the wrong technique can escalate rather than de-escalate a behavior problem. For example, touch control for some students with AS appears to drain off frustration. That is, by merely touching the student's shoulder, the teacher can feel an immediate relaxation on the part of the student. But another student might be startled by a touch because he (a) did not know the teacher was going to enter his space, (b) misperceived touch as an aggression, or (c) perceived touch as discomforting or painful due to sensory issues. Thus, in these cases, touch control would have the opposite effect of the one intended.

Interventions at this stage do not require extensive teacher time, but it is important for teachers to watch for and understand the events that precipitate the target behaviors so they can (a) be ready to intervene early or (b) teach students strategies to maintain self-control during these times. Please note, however, that students cannot be taught these strategies when they are in the rumbling stage!

Interventions at this stage are merely band-aids. They do not teach students to recognize their own frustration or provide a means of handling it. As mentioned earlier, such efforts must take place during teachable moments (see Figure 2.1).

Adult Behavior During the Rumbling Stage

As illustrated in Figure 2.1, as the student's behavior escalates, the adult's behavior usually follows. Thus, teachers or parents must realize that they may be experiencing their own rumbling behaviors when the child begins the cycle. It is imperative that the adults remain calm so they can focus on helping the child leave the cycle. Most important, the adult must prevent a power struggle between himself and the child because when the struggle begins, the adult has "lost."

During the rumbling stage, it is almost impossible for the child to be flexible unless this behavior has been taught and is firmly entrenched in the child's repertoire. During this stage, the adult must re-evaluate the student's goals and be flexible so that the child can meet the "new" goal: to get back to the teachable moment. The behaviors shown in Table 2.3 can be effective for adults.

Table 2.3 Effective Adult Behaviors During the Rumbling Stage	
1. Remain calm	4. Prevent power struggle
2. Use a quiet voice	5. Re-evaluate student goals
3. Take deep breaths	6. Be flexible – the child cannot

Just as it is important to understand interventions that may diffuse a crisis, it is important to know which teacher behaviors are likely to escalate behavior problems. The list of behaviors in Table 2.4 are almost certain to turn a potential crisis into a meltdown (Albert, 1989).

Rage Stage

If student behavior is not diffused during the rumbling stage, a tantrum, rage, or meltdown is likely to occur.

Child Behavior During the Rage Stage

At this point, the student is disinhibited and acts impulsively, emotionally, and sometimes explosively. Behaviors may include screaming, biting, hitting,

Table 2.4
Adult Behaviors That Can Escalate a Crisis

- Raising voice or yelling
- Making assumptions
- Preaching
- Backing the student into a corner
- Saying "I'm the boss here"
- Pleading or bribing
- Insisting on having the last word
- Bringing up unrelated events
- Using tense body language
- Generalizing by making remarks such as "You kids are all the same"
- Using sarcasm
- Attacking the student's character
- Making unsubstantiated accusations
- Nagging
- Holding a grudge

- Acting superior
- Throwing a temper tantrum
- Using unwarranted physical force
- Mimicking the child or youth
- Drawing unrelated persons into the conflict
- Making comparisons with siblings, other students, etc.
- Insisting that the adult is right
- Having a double standard: "Do what I say, not what I do"
- Commanding, demanding, dominating
- Rewarding the student for unacceptable behavior
- Using degrading, insulting, humiliating or embarrassing putdowns

kicking, destroying property, or self-injury. Another type of rage may also manifest itself, internal rage. The student may become so upset that she completely withdraws, unable to verbalize or act in a rational manner (see Table 2.5).

Since no effective prevention can take place during this stage, emphasis should be placed on student, peer, and teacher safety as well as protection of

Table 2.5
Typical Rage Stage Behaviors

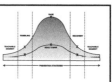

1. Disinhibited
2. Acting impulsively
3. Emotional
4. Explosive
5. Destroying property
6. Self-injurious
7. Screaming
8. Biting
9. Hitting
10. Kicking
11. Internalizing behavior

school, home, or personal property. The best way to cope with the rage is to get the child to a cool zone, but only if she can be moved without physical assistance greater than a gentle touch. The cool zone may be the room in which the behavior occurs, free of materials that can be destroyed and of other children who may unintentionally be harmed. Or it may be a room equipped by an occupational therapist with objects that help the child calm down and relax, such as a trampoline. Above all, the room must not be viewed as a reward or a disciplinary room, but should be seen as a place where the student can go to regain self-control. If the child has a meltdown in front of peers, it is often easier to remove the other children. However, to do so, a plan must be in place (see Student Crisis Plan Sheet, pages 59-61), and assistance must be obtained to support the child with AS or the other students during relocation.

Some children manifest rage by raising their voice or yelling at the teacher or caretaker. It is important that adults not engage in this type of banter with the child. It may be helpful to indicate to the child that you cannot talk and then to set a timer to signal that you will talk with the child when the timer goes off and the child is calm.

Generally, adults should be nonconfrontational and use few words as this can minimize the occurrence of power struggles. Children at the rage stage are not thinking – they are reacting – so words have little meaning. As in the rumbling stage, it is important to re-evaluate your goal for the student and be flexible. The ultimate goal for the child at this stage is to get him to the recovery stage. Table 2.6 lists a series of interventions found to be helpful during the rage stage.

Table 2.6
Rage Stage Interventions

1. Protect the student	9. Obtain assistance
2. Protect the environment	10. Prompt to a cool zone, as
3. Protect others	appropriate
4. Don't discipline	11. Use few words
5. Remove the audience	12. Prevent a power struggle
6. Be nonconfrontational	13. Re-evaluate the student's goals
7. Plan a "graceful" exit strategy	14. Be flexible – the child cannot
8. Follow a plan	15. Set a timer

Meltdowns are not purposeful, and once the rage stage begins, it most often must run its course. Adams (1997) related a rage incident involving a young boy,

> The first meltdown for one young man occurred while in a parking lot. A stranger swore at him and called him a 'stupid kid.' The boy started to shake a mailbox, and began to kick and scream. ... It was noted by the parent that during later attacks, the boy would sometimes say, 'I don't want to do this!' It appeared that he could not disengage from the emotion, once it had started. (p. 72)

Priority should be placed on helping the student regain control and preserving her dignity. Teachers should have developed plans for (a) obtaining assistance from educators such as a crisis teacher or principal, (b) removing other students from the area, or (c) providing therapeutic restraint, if necessary. The Student Crisis Plan Sheet (see pages 59-61) is helpful in formulating this tactic.

Adult Behavior During the Rage Cycle

When we find ourselves in situations considered very uncomfortable or dangerous, it is natural to experience a "flight or fight" reaction. When working with a child who is in the rage stage of the cycle, it is not uncommon for an adult to experience this phenomenon. It is essential that the teacher or parent remain calm – deep breathing can help attain this state. According to Hubbard (personal communication, 2004), the strategy "less is more" is important for adults to remember during this stage. In other words, the fewer words ... the better, and the fewer gestures ... the better. The adult should not take the student's words personally during this stage. It is important to think that the child's mouth is on "automatic pilot," saying words that are unplanned and not meant. Adults should disengage emotionally by, for example, creating a lesson plan mentally, planning a grocery list, etc. (see Table 2.7).

Table 2.7
Effective Adult Behaviors
During the Rage Stage

1. Control "flight or fight" tendency
2. Remember that less is more
3. Remain calm and quiet
4. Do not take behaviors personally
5. Disengage emotionally
6. Be conscious of your nonverbal cues
7. Take deep breaths

Recovery Stage

Although many believe that the crisis cycle ends with the rage stage, this is not the case. As shown in Figure 2.1, there is also a third stage: the recovery stage.

Child Behavior During the Recovery Stage

Following the meltdown, the child may have contrite feelings and apologize, often without full recall of the meltdown behavior. Or he may become sullen, withdraw, or deny that inappropriate behavior occurred. Some children are so physically exhausted after a meltdown that they need to sleep (see Table 2.8). Children at this stage are considered fragile. If they are not given significant time to calm down after the meltdown, children often enter the cycle again and experience a shortened rumbling stage that quickly escalates to the rage stage.

Table 2.8 Typical Recovery Behaviors	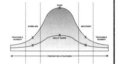
• Sleeping • Withdrawal into fantasy • Denial of rage behaviors • Apologizing	

Note. Consider the child to be fragile. She can re-enter the cycle easily at this stage.

If the child is physically exhausted, he may need to sleep. Most often at this stage, the child is not ready to learn – he is not in a teachable moment. Thus, it is important that teachers work with students to help them to once again become a part of the classroom routine or structure. Typically, this is best accomplished by directing the student to a highly motivating task or one that she can easily accomplish. In addition, many students need their "space" and are most comfortable when being allowed to work independently. Others may require the comfort of an adult nearby. Knowing the individual child or youth will help adults use the appropriate strategy. A list of recovery interventions is presented in Table 2.9. Again, this is not rewarding "bad"(!) behavior; rather it helps the child or youth return to a "teachable state."

This is *not* the time to discuss the rage behavior with the child or attempt to teach a relaxation strategy. The child can use a relaxation strategy only if it was learned and practiced earlier during a teachable moment. As mentioned, a good rule of thumb for interventions during this stage is to use only interventions that are not cognitively draining for the student and that the student can perform with some degree of automaticity. (Skills may be considered automatic if they were taught, practiced, and mastered during teachable moments.)

Table 2.9
Recovery Stage Interventions

1. Allow to sleep, if necessary
2. Support use of relaxation techniques
3. Do not refer to the rage behavior
4. Support with structure
5. Consider the child "fragile"
6. Plan instructional interventions to provide alternatives to tantrums, rage, meltdowns, and shut-downs

7. Determine appropriate option for child:
   - Redirect to successful activity or special interest
   - Provide space
   - Ensure that interventions are presented at or below the child's functioning level
8. Check to see if student is ready to learn
9. Do not make excessive demands

Adult Behavior During the Recovery Stage

Both the child and the adult experiencing the rage stage are impacted. Thus, adults working with children with AS who have meltdowns must be aware that they need to take time to recover also. While it is often not possible for a teacher or parent to take time to relax and refocus immediately after a child's rage, it is important that the adult schedule time for recovery at some point (see Table 2.10). If the meltdown occurs at school, the teacher may attempt to relax in the teacher's lounge when her students go to music. At home, the father who was with the child during the meltdown may go out for a drive while the mother stays at home with the child. Perhaps after the child goes to bed, the mother who helped the child through the rage and recovery stage can take a soothing bath. It is important that adults who live or work with children and youth with AS realize that they need to be at their personal best to give best effort to these individuals.

Table 2.10
Effective Adult Behaviors
During the Recovery Stage

1. Remain calm and quiet
2. Take time for yourself to regroup

Countercontrol

The concept of countercontrol is important to understand when working with students who experience tantrums, rage, and meltdowns. Many children and youth with AS do not cope well when faced with control by adults, so they may try to countercontrol. That is, the children may take steps (sometimes subconsciously) to be in control. According to Carey and Bourbon (2004),

> ... behaviors that are problematic for people who work with children might be countercontrol in disguise. When people describe a child's behavior with certain words – *noncompliant, disobedient, resistant, wilful, persistent, stubborn, oppositional, rebellious* – countercontrol may be lurking. In fact, any time a student's behavior frustrates your attempts to see that student acting in a particular way, you could be experiencing countercontrol. (p. 4)

The more teachers try to control students, the more some students try to countercontrol. The following tend to promote countercontrol behaviors: (a) tightening reinforcement contingencies, (b) introducing time-out, and (c) assuming more stringent punishments.

Countercontrol is minimized when students perceive they have choices, understand why they are learning specific skills, and their interests are incorporated in their curriculum. Compromise and negotiation opportunities also lessen the occurrence of countercontrol. Carey and Bourbon (2004) pose three questions that teachers should ask to help determine if they are too controlling:

1. When you are teaching, do you ever get frustrated or angry?
2. With some students, do you find that the more you try to direct them, the more difficult they become?
3. Do you sometimes feel like students are manipulating you and that they often seem to enjoy seeing you become upset? (pp. 8-9)

Affirmative responses to these questions may mean that adults working or living with a child with AS may be too controlling and, therefore, need to re-evaluate their teaching goals to reduce their controlling behaviors. This will, in turn, reduce countercontrol in students.

Teachable Moments

Our ultimate goal when working with children and youth with AS who experience the rage cycle is to prevent it from occurring. This can happen by teaching the student to understand her environment and herself by using tools that support academic, social, sensory, and behavioral success, and by structuring the environment for success. That is, the emphasis is on *preventing* the cycle from occurring. Structure for home and school helps ensure that rage does not occur. Initially, when the child begins the rumbling stage, the adult must recognize the student's rumbling behaviors and intervene to help the child return to the teachable moment. We must do everything in our power to prevent the rage stage. This is the *ultimate* goal. While initially adults must recognize the behaviors in the child that indicate rumbling and intervene, we must also teach the student to recognize in himself the rumbling behaviors and what he can do to move himself to a teachable moment. This generally takes considerable time and effort.

The ONLY time a child can learn a skill – whether academic, social, behavioral, or sensory – is during a teachable moment. Thus, considerable effort must be placed on *preventing* the occurrence of tantrums, rage, and meltdowns so the child is available to learn. For example, Miguel enters the rumbling stage each time he is given an assignment from a new unit in the math book. His rumbling behaviors include talking to himself, rocking in his chair, and erasing his paper so hard that a hole starts to appear. He escalates to the rage stage by wadding up his paper, throwing it on the floor, and crying. Because he has problems modulating or changing his behavior, once he becomes upset, for all practical purposes, intervention is too late.

Miguel's teacher, Mr. Hagen, needs to re-evaluate his goals for Miguel. For example, Mr. Hagen must ask himself, "If Miguel rumbles with a math assignment from a new unit, what can I do to help him begin a new assignment without entering this stage?" A three-pronged approach like the following is often effective: (a) teach Miguel how to recognize rumbling behaviors in himself, (b) provide strategies that can help Miguel calm himself *before* an assignment is given and to remain calm *during* the assignment, and (c) plan a schedule of reinforcers designed to build self-esteem and help Miguel to tackle new assignments successfully.

Mr. Hagen may decide it is prudent not to introduce new math assignments to Miguel while he works with him on the first two goals. Then when Miguel has mastered (a) and (b) and understands the reinforcers in place and feels confident in himself (c), Mr. Hagen will then introduce a new math unit and a single math problem that he knows Miguel can complete. When Miguel is successful using this approach, Mr. Hagen can gradually increase the number of problems that Miguel is to do in new units. This systematic approach will help

Miguel learn new skills. However, if Mr. Hagen had kept presenting new math items without re-evaluating his goals, both Miguel and he would become frustrated with Miguel's rumbling and his subsequent rage behaviors.

To effectively carry out individualized interventions with children and adolescents with AS, we must analyze the behaviors that precede situations, as well as those that happen during and after. Instead of random, hit-or-miss efforts, parents and educators have at their disposal a series of tools whereby they can rather closely pinpoint behaviors and their causes. In the following chapter, we will look more closely at functional assessment of behavior with particular emphasis on its use with children and adolescents with AS and difficult moments.

Functional Assessment of Behavior

Each student displays unique behaviors throughout the rage cycle. Understanding behaviors at each stage helps teachers or parents plan interventions that can prevent or de-escalate a potential meltdown. As mentioned in Chapter 2, student behaviors typically do not occur in isolation or randomly; they are most often associated with a reason or cause. In short, the student who engages in an inappropriate behavior is attempting to communicate something.

Before selecting interventions, it is important to understand the function or role a given behavior plays. *Functional assessment* is designed to ask the question, "Why does Johnny *need* to do _____?" As such, it is a first step in developing effective interventions. Indeed, without determining the reasons, causes, or conditions under which a behavior occurs, interventions are not likely to be effective. The following six steps comprise a functional assessment:

1. Identify and describe student behavior.
2. Describe setting demands and antecedents.
3. Collect baseline data and/or work samples.
4. Complete functional analysis measures and develop a hypothesis.
5. Develop and implement a behavioral intervention plan.
6. Collect data and follow up to analyze the effectiveness of the plan.

The remainder of this chapter will look more closely at each of these steps.

Identifying and Describing Student Behavior

Most basic to the process of functional assessment is identifying and describing the behavior on which an intervention is to be structured. When examining the student's role in the rage cycle, it is important to clearly define the behavior or behaviors that are evident. Behaviors must be stated in observable terms so that everyone who comes in contact with the child recognizes the same behaviors. If student behaviors are not clearly defined, we run the risk that not all educators will recognize the behavior and, thus, will not apply the designated interventions correctly and at the appropriate time. A behavior identified as "the student shows stress," for example, does little to help the fourth-grade teacher understand when the student with AS is entering the rage cycle. To be effective, definitions should use verbs with information on how a behavior is performed, how often if occurs, and its duration and intensity. Thus, the teacher who observes "the student under stress begins to pace rapidly back and forth while whispering" can easily recognize the behavior.

Describing Setting Demands and Antecedents

Before designing an intervention, it is important to understand the environment(s) in which the behaviors are likely to occur. The Autism Asperger Resource Center (1997) designed a checklist that helps describe the classroom environment by asking specific questions regarding (a) teaching methods, (b) grading, (c) tests, (d) teaching materials, (e) product requirements, (f) student behavior, (g) class management, and (h) class structure. All of these components are integral to understanding why a behavior may be occurring (see Figure 3.1).

Other factors related to setting demands include time factors, instructional expectations, behavioral expectations, and social demands.

Collecting Baseline Data and/or Work Samples

Concurrent with describing setting demands and antecedents, the student must be observed in different environments. Observation data, an important component of the functional assessment process, should be collected to document behavior frequency, duration, and/or intensity (Janzen, 2003; Kerr & Nelson, 1993). It is extremely important that behavioral data be collected both in the environments where the behavior occurs and where it does not occur. In addition, permanent products or work samples should be analyzed to determine student achievement rate across academic settings as a clue to behavioral manifestations.

Assessing the Setting Demands in the Classroom

Name: _____ Class: _____ Date: _____

Please complete this questionnaire to help us support instruction in your class.
Circle the number that best answers each question.

TEACHING METHODS	Never	Sometimes	Always
A. % of class time spent in lecture .... _____%			
B. % of class time spent in discussion .... _____%			
C. % of learning done through independent study .... _____%			
D. % of time in cooperative learning groups .... _____%			
E. Is there a consistent daily routine? 1	2 - 3	4	5
F. Is there a consistent weekly routine? 1	2 3	4	5

COMMENTS: _____

_____

GRADES	Never	Sometimes	Always
A. Is extra credit work accepted and/or encouraged? 1	2 3	4	5
B. Can students rework previous assignments? 1	2 3	4	5
C. Is the grading criteria established and posted at the beginning of the course? 1	2 3	4	5

COMMENTS: _____

_____

TESTS	Never	Sometimes	Always
A. Is a variety of test methods used in your class? 1	2 3	4	5
1. Multiple-choice tests? 1	2 3	4	5
2. Essay tests? 1	2 3	4	5
3. Matching tests? 1	2 3	4	5
4. True/false tests? 1	2 3	4	5
5. Open book tests? 1	2 3	4	5
6. Take-home tests? 1	2 3	4	5
7. Group/cooperative tests? 1	2 3	4	5
B. Are tests given in your class? 1	2 3	4	5
1. Daily tests? 1	2 3	4	5
2. Weekly tests? 1	2 3	4	5
3. Monthly tests? 1	2 3	4	5
4. Quarterly tests? 1	2 3	4	5
C. Do you allow test taking assistance for students? 1	2 3	4	5

COMMENTS: _____

_____

Figure 3.1. Setting demands checklist.

TEACHING MATERIALS	Never	Sometimes		Always
A. Do you use a textbook? 1	2	3	4	5
B. Do you use handouts? 1	2	3	4	5
C. Do students need to bring outside materials to class? .. 1	2	3	4	5

List materials needed: _____

D. Are prerequisite skills required? 1	2	3	4	5

List skills: _____

E. Are typing/word processing skills required? 1	2	3	4	5

COMMENTS: _____

WRITTEN & OTHER MAJOR PRODUCTS	Never	Sometimes		Always
A. Are students required to write in complete sentences? .. 1	2	3	4	5
B. Are students required to write paragraphs? 1	2	3	4	5
C. Are students required to write essays or 3-5 paragraphs?.....................................1	2	3	4	5
D. Is a research paper required? 1	2	3	4	5
E. Is an oral presentation required? 1	2	3	4	5
F. Are there any required major course projects/assignments?.............................1	2	3	4	5

List: _____

G. How often do you require students to answer questions in written form? 1	2	3	4	5

COMMENTS: _____

STUDENT BEHAVIOR	Never	Sometimes		Always
A. Is on-time behavior factored into the grade? 1	2	3	4	5
B. Is attendance factored into the grade? 1	2	3	4	5
C. Is student participation factored into the grade? 1	2	3	4	5
D. Is work completion factored into the grade?...........1	2	3	4	5
E. Are other student behaviors factored into the grade? ... 1	2	3	4	5

List behaviors (i.e., on-task behavior, listening, etc.): _____

F. Is student notetaking an important part of your class? .. 1	2	3	4	5
G. Are students expected to manage their out-of-class behavior independently? 1	2	3	4	5

COMMENTS: _____

Figure 3.1. Continued

CLASS MANAGEMENT   Never   Sometimes Always

A. Are rules and guidelines posted and
   reviewed in your classroom?........................1   2   3   4   5
B. Are consequences clearly communicated to the students?. 1   2   3   4   5
C. Do you use material reinforcements?.................1   2   3   4   5
D. Do you use other reinforcements? 1   2   3   4   5
   List: _____

COMMENTS: _____

_____

CLASSROOM STRUCTURE   Never   Sometimes Always

A. What is your present classroom seating arrangement?
   Draw a quick picture.

            Example   Your room

```
        T
    S  S  S  S  S
    S  S  S  S  S
    S  S  S  S  S
```

B. How often are students in the above
   seating arrangements? 1   2   3   4   5
C. What other alternate arrangements do you use?

   Draw a quick picture.

D. How often are students in the above alternate
   seating arrangements? 1   2   3   4   5

COMMENTS: _____

_____

Figure 3.1. **Continued**

Used with the permission of the Autism Asperger Resource Center, 3901 Rainbow Blvd., Kansas City, KS 66160-7335, 913/588-5988, fax 913/588-5942 (www.KUMC.edu/AARC).

Completing Functional Analysis Measures and Developing a Hypothesis

To most effectively and efficiently intervene with a problem behavior, it is important to understand the cause, triggers, or functions of the behavior. The goal of functional assessment and related intervention procedures is not simply to eradicate a behavior, but to help the student learn new and more appropriate ways of ensuring her needs are met.

The list of possible behavior functions or triggers is numerous and may include (a) escape/avoidance; (b) attention from peers or adults; (c) anger or stress expression; (d) emotional state, such as depression, frustration or confusion; (e) power/control; (f) intimidation; (g) sensory stimulation; (g) fear or relief of fear; (h) requesting or obtaining something (e.g., food, activity, object, comfort, routine, social interaction); or (i) expression of internal stimulation (e.g., sinus pain, skin irritation, hunger).

Other triggers for children with AS include (a) obsessional thoughts, (b) fear of failure, (c) fear related to self-esteem (i.e., loss of face, loss of perceived position), or (d) the need to protect an irrational thought.

In addition, issues related to the curriculum may also cause behavioral issues such as:
- activities that take a long time to complete
- activities the child dislikes
- activities with unclear completion criteria
- activities perceived as irrelevant by the child
- few opportunities to clarify instructions
- lack of predictability
- inadequate assistance on assignments
- few opportunities to communicate
- activities that are too easy or too difficult
  (Carr, Reeve, & Magito-McLaughlin, 1996).

Environmental issues such as the following can also be related to meltdowns: (a) high noise level, (b) uncomfortable temperature, (c) poor seating arrangements, (d) and frequent disruptions.

Finally, physiological factors cannot be overlooked when determining the cause of meltdowns and ways to prevent them. These may include (a) hunger or thirst; (b) medication side effects; (c) allergies/sickness; (d) fatigue; and (e) being upset due to a fight, missing the bus, or a disruptive routine (Kern, Dunlap, Clarke, & Childs, 1994).

Understanding which of these functions a given behavior serves is one of the initial steps in setting up an effective intervention. Several functional assessment instruments are available commercially to help teachers and parents identify behavior functions or triggers (see Figure 3. 2 for sample copies of some of these instruments).

Motivation Assessment Scale
by V. Mark Durand and Daniel B. Crimmins

Name _____ Rater _____ Date _____

Behavior Description _____

Setting Description _____

ITEM	RESPONSE						
	NEVER	ALMOST NEVER	SELDOM	HALF THE TIME	USUALLY	ALMOST ALWAYS	ALWAYS
1. Would the behavior occur continuously, over and over, if this person was left alone for long periods of time? (For example, several hours.)	0	1	2	3	4	5	6
2. Does the behavior occur following a request to perform a difficult task?	0	1	2	3	4	5	6
3. Does the behavior seem to occur in response to your talking to other persons in the room?	0	1	2	3	4	5	6
4. Does the behavior ever occur to get a toy, food or activity that this person has been told that he or she can't have?	0	1	2	3	4	5	6
5. Would the behavior occur repeatedly, in the same way, for very long periods of time, if no one was around? (For example, rocking back and forth for over an hour.)	0	1	2	3	4	5	6
6. Does the behavior occur when any request is made of this person?	0	1	2	3	4	5	6
7. Does the behavior occur whenever you stop attending to this person?	0	1	2	3	4	5	6
8. Does the behavior occur when you take away a favorite toy, food, or activity?	0	1	2	3	4	5	6
9. Does it appear to you that this person enjoys performing the behavior? (It feels, tastes, looks, smells, and/or sounds pleasing.)	0	1	2	3	4	5	6
10. Does this person seem to do the behavior to upset or annoy you when you are trying to get him or her to do what you ask?	0	1	2	3	4	5	6

Figure 3.2. Functional assessment instruments: *Motivation Assessment Scale.*

ITEM	RESPONSE

	NEVER	ALMOST NEVER	SELDOM	HALF THE TIME	USUALLY	ALMOST ALWAYS	ALWAYS
11. Does this person seem to do the behavior to upset or annoy you when you are not paying attention to him or her? (For example, if you are sitting in a separate room, interacting with another person.)	0	1	2	3	4	5	6
12. Does the behavior stop occurring shortly after you give this person the toy, food or activity he or she has requested?	0	1	2	3	4	5	6
13. When the behavior is occurring, does this person seem calm and unaware of anything else going on around him or her?	0	1	2	3	4	5	6
14. Does the behavior stop occurring shortly after (one to five minutes) you stop working or making demands of this person?	0	1	2	3	4	5	6
15. Does this person seem to do the behavior to get you to spend some time with him or her?	0	1	2	3	4	5	6
16. Does the behavior seem to occur when this person has been told that he or she can't do something he or she had wanted to do?	0	1	2	3	4	5	6

SCORING

	Sensory	Escape	Attention	Tangible
	1. ___	2. ___	3. ___	4. ___
	5. ___	6. ___	7. ___	8. ___
	9. ___	10. ___	11. ___	12. ___
	13. ___	14. ___	15. ___	16. ___
Total score =	___	___	___	___
Mean score =	___	___	___	___
Relative ranking =	___	___	___	___

Figure 3.2. Continued

Problem Behavior Questionnaire

RESPONDENT INFORMATION

Student _____ DOB _____ Grade _____ Sex M F   IEP: Y N

Teacher _____ School _____

Telephone _____ Date _____

STUDENT BEHAVIOR

Please briefly describe the problem behavior(s)

DIRECTIONS: Keeping in mind a typical episode of the problem behavior, circle the frequency at which each of the following statements is true.

	Never	10% of the time	25% of the time	50% of the time	75% of the time	90% of the time	All of the time
1. Does the problem behavior occur and persist when you make a request to perform a task?	0	1	2	3	4	5	6
2. When the problem behavior occurs do you redirect the student to get back to task or follow rules?	0	1	2	3	4	5	6
3. During a conflict with peers, if the student engages in the problem behavior do peers leave the student alone?	0	1	2	3	4	5	6
4. When the problem behavior occurs do peers verbally respond or laugh at the student?	0	1	2	3	4	5	6

Figure 3.2. Functional assessment instruments: *Problem Behavior Questionnaire.*

	Never	10% of the time	25% of the time	50% of the time	75% of the time	90% of the time	All of the time
5. Is the problem behavior more likely to occur following a conflict outside of the classroom? (e.g., bus write-up)	0	1	2	3	4	5	6
6. Does the problem behavior occur to get your attention when you are working with other students?	0	1	2	3	4	5	6
7. Does the problem behavior occur in the presence of specific peers?	0	1	2	3	4	5	6
8. Is the problem behavior more likely to continue to occur throughout the day following an earlier episode?	0	1	2	3	4	5	6
9. Does the problem behavior occur during specific academic activities?	0	1	2	3	4	5	6
10. Does the problem behavior stop when peers stop interacting with the student?	0	1	2	3	4	5	6
11. Does the behavior occur when peers are attending to other students?	0	1	2	3	4	5	6
12. If the student engages in the problem behavior do you provide 1-to-1 instruction to get student back on task?	0	1	2	3	4	5	6
13. Will the student stop doing the problem behavior if you stop making requests or end an academic activity?	0	1	2	3	4	5	6
14. If the student engages in the problem behavior, do peers stop interacting with the student?	0	1	2	3	4	5	6
15. Is the problem behavior more likely to occur following unscheduled events or disruptions in classroom routines?	0	1	2	3	4	5	6

Figure 3.2. Continued

Problem Behavior Questionnaire Profile

DIRECTIONS: Circle the score given for each question from the scale below the corresponding question number (in bold).

PEERS						ADULTS						SETTING EVENTS		
Escape			Attention			Escape			Attention					
3	**10**	**14**	**4**	**7**	**11**	**1**	**9**	**13**	**2**	**6**	**12**	**5**	**8**	**15**
6	6	6	6	6	6	6	6	6	6	6	6	6	6	6
5	5	5	5	5	5	5	5	5	5	5	5	5	5	5
4	4	4	4	4	4	4	4	4	4	4	4	4	4	4
3	3	3	3	3	3	3	3	3	3	3	3	3	3	3
2	2	2	2	2	2	2	2	2	2	2	2	2	2	2
1	1	1	1	1	1	1	1	1	1	1	1	1	1	1
0	0	0	0	0	0	0	0	0	0	0	0	0	0	0

Figure 3.2. Continued

Lewis, T. J., Scott, T. M., & Sugai, G. (1994). The problem behavior questionnaire: A teacher-based instrument to develop functional hypotheses of problem behavior in general education classrooms. *Diagnostique, 19*(2-3), 103-115. Reprinted with permission.

Student-Assisted
Functional-Assessment Interview

Student _____

Date _____

Interviewer _____

SECTION I

1. In general, is your work too hard for you?   ALWAYS   SOMETIMES   NEVER

2. In general, is your work too easy for you?   ALWAYS   SOMETIMES   NEVER

3. When you ask for help appropriately,
   do you get it?   ALWAYS   SOMETIMES   NEVER

4. Do you think work periods for each
   subject are too long?   ALWAYS   SOMETIMES   NEVER

5. Do you think work periods for each
   subject are too short?   ALWAYS   SOMETIMES   NEVER

6. When you do seatwork, do you do better
   when someone works with you?   ALWAYS   SOMETIMES   NEVER

7. Do you think people notice when
   you do a good job?   ALWAYS   SOMETIMES   NEVER

8. Do you think you get the points or
   rewards you deserve when you
   do good work?   ALWAYS   SOMETIMES   NEVER

9. Do you think you would do better in
   school if you received more rewards?   ALWAYS   SOMETIMES   NEVER

10. In general, do you find your
    work interesting?   ALWAYS   SOMETIMES   NEVER

11. Are there things in the classroom that
    distract you?   ALWAYS   SOMETIMES   NEVER

12. Is your work challenging enough for you?   ALWAYS   SOMETIMES   NEVER

SECTION II

1. When do you think you have the fewest problems with _____ in school?

   Why do you not have problems during this/these time(s)?

Figure 3.2. Functional assessment instruments: *Student-Assisted Functional-Assessment Interview.*

2. When do you think you have the most problems with _____ in school?

   Why do you have problems during this/these time(s)?

3. What changes could be made so you would have fewer problems with _____ ?

4. What kinds of rewards would you like to earn for good behavior or good school work?

5. What are your favorite activities at school?

6. What are your hobbies or interests?

7. If you had the chance, what activities would you like to do that you don't have the opportunity to do?

SECTION III

Rate how much you like the following subjects:

	not at all		fair		very much
Reading	1	2	3	4	5
Math	1	2	3	4	5
Spelling	1	2	3	4	5
Handwriting	1	2	3	4	5
Science	1	2	3	4	5
English	1	2	3	4	5
Music	1	2	3	4	5
PE	1	2	3	4	5
Computers	1	2	3	4	5
Art	1	2	3	4	5

Figure 3.2. **Continued**

SECTION IV

What do you like about Reading?

What don't you like about Reading?

What do you like about Math?

What don't you like about Math?

What do you like about Spelling?

What don't you like about Spelling?

What do you like about Handwriting?

What don't you like about Handwriting?

What do you like about Science?

What don't you like about Science?

What do you like about Social Studies?

What don't you like about Social Studies?

What do you like about English?

What don't you like about English?

What do you like about Music?

What don't you like about Music?

What do you like about PE?

What don't you like about PE?

What do you like about Computers?

What don't you like about Computers?

What do you like about Art?

What don't you like about Art?

Figure 3.2. Continued

Kern, L., Dunlap, G., Clarke, S., & Childs, K. (1994). Student-assisted functional assessment interview. *Diagnostique, 19*(2-3), 29-39. Reprinted with permission.

Instead of relying on commercial instruments that are not tailor-made for their school environment and culture, many school districts have created tools that are effective in identifying behavior function. For example, McConnell, Hilvitz, and Cox (1998) designed a functional assessment and data collection packet for their school district (see Figure 3.3).

Behavioral Intervention Plan

Student _____   School _____

Date Developed_____   Date Implemented_____

Grade_____

Baseline Data Results:

Hypothesis Statement:

Person(s) Responsible for Implementing Plan:

DESCRIPTION OF THE BEHAVIOR:

Behavior	Behavior Defined

INTERVENTION GOAL:

Figure 3.3. Sample behavioral intervention plan.

INTERVENTION PLAN:

1.

2.

3.

4.

5.

WHEN AND WHERE THE PLAN WILL BE IMPLEMENTED:

Figure 3.3. Continued

INTERVENTION DATA COLLECTION SUMMARY:

_____

_____

FOLLOW-UP AND REVIEW DATE(S):

COMMENTS:

TEAM MEETING PARTICIPANTS:

Name	Position

Figure 3.3. Continued

McConnell, M., Hilvitz, P., & Cox, C. J. (1997). *Behavioral intervention plan.* Developed for Turner Unified School District #202, Kansas City, KS. Reprinted with permission.

Developing and Implementing a Behavioral Intervention Plan

Once functional assessment data have been collected, reviewed, and analyzed, the information must be assimilated to gain a thorough understanding of a child's rage cycle. This process is important because the cycle most often reveals a pattern and, therefore, provides important information for future interventions. The typical pattern of a meltdown is as follows:

- The cycle occurs for a reason.
- Each episode is preceded by a reason or reasons (often called a *trigger* or *set of triggers*).
- The build-up to the tantrum, rage, or meltdown is typically manifested in the same way across episodes.
- Each episode lasts approximately the same length of time.
- Recovery may or may not look the same after each meltdown,

Once the data have been analyzed and each of these issues has been defined, it is time to write a behavioral intervention plan. This plan includes a written description of specific interventions to use with a given student to promote behavioral, social, and academic success. In addition, the persons who will be responsible for implementing the plan must be identified and listed.

As an accompaniment to a behavioral intervention plan, the Student Crisis Plan Sheet (see Figure 3.4) is a useful tool for specifying student behaviors and appropriate interventions for each stage in the rage cycle. This form helps educators and parents (a) develop a blueprint of events that are likely to precipitate rage, (b) identify behaviors the student exhibits at each stage of the rage cycle, and (c) outline interventions that can be used at each stage to help the student regain behavioral control. The form is also helpful in ensuring that everyone involved is following the same plan to help the student exert positive control over her environment.

Collecting Data and Following up to Analyze the Effectiveness of the Plan

Whenever the student engages in behaviors that are a part of the rage cycle, a Crisis Report Form should be completed (see Figure 3.5). This form documents student behaviors as well as interventions implemented at each stage, including their effectiveness. Educators and parents should meet according to a predetermined schedule to compare the student's baseline data to intervention data and information summarized on the Crisis Report

Student Crisis Plan Sheet

Student Name _____   Student Age/Grade _____

Teacher Name _____   Date of Plan _____

ENVIRONMENTAL/PERSONNEL CONSIDERATIONS

1. Describe how you can obtain assistance when it is needed _____
_____
_____

2. At which stage should outside assistance be sought?

_____ rumbling   _____ rage   _____ recovery

3. Which school personnel are available to provide assistance?

_____ principal   _____ school psychologist   _____ paraprofessional
_____ social worker   _____ counselor
_____ other (please specify) _____
_____ other (please specify) _____

4. Where should child(ren) exit to? (specify room or school) _____

5. At what stage should the plan be used by others in the classroom?

_____ rumbling   _____ rage   _____ recovery

6. Are there any extenuating circumstances that others should know about this
student (i.e., medications, related medical conditions, home situation)?

7. Who should be notified of the incident? _____

8. How should the incident be documented? _____

Figure 3.4. **Student crisis plan sheet.**

RUMBLING STAGE

1. What environmental factors/activities or antecedents lead to "rumbling" behaviors?

____ unplanned change ____ difficult assignment ____ crowds
____ teacher criticism ____ transitions ____ conflict with classmate
____ other (please describe) _____

2. What behaviors does the student exhibit during the rumbling stage?

____ bites nails ____ tenses muscles ____ stares
____ taunts others ____ refuses to work ____ fidgets
____ other (please describe) _____
____ other (please describe) _____

3. Does the student mention any of the following complaints or illness?

____ stomachache ____ headache ____ not applicable
____ other (please describe) _____

4. Should the student be sent to the nurse if there is a complaint of illness?

____ yes ____ no

5. How long does the rumbling stage last before it progresses to the next stage?

_____

6. What interventions should be used at this stage?

____ antiseptic bouncing ____ proximity control ____ touch control
____ "just walk and don't talk" ____ home base ____ redirecting
____ other (please specify) _____
_____
____ other (please specify) _____
_____

Figure 3.4. Continued

RAGE STAGE

1. What behaviors does the student exhibit during the rage stage?

_____ student verbally lashes out at teacher

_____ student verbally lashes out at other students

_____ student threatens to hit teacher

_____ student threatens to hit students

_____ student destroys materials

_____ student attempts to leave classroom

_____ student withdraws from teacher

_____ student hurts self

_____ other (please specify) _____

_____ other (please specify) _____

2. What teacher interventions should be used during this stage?

_____ physically move child to safe room

_____ prompt child to move to safe room

_____ remove others from the classroom

_____ redirect student

_____ other (please specify) _____

_____ other (please specify) _____

3. What is the role of others in the child's environment during the rage stage?_____

_____

_____

RECOVERY STAGE

1. What behaviors does the student exhibit during the recovery stage without intervention?

_____ sullenness   _____ withdrawal into fantasy   _____ denial

_____ "typical" student behavior

_____ other (please describe) _____

_____ other (please describe) _____

2. What supportive techniques should be used during this stage?_____

_____

_____

3. What interventions should be used at a later time to assist the student in gaining more self-control?_____

_____

_____

Figure 3.4. **Continued**

Crisis Report Form

Student Name _____

Teacher Name _____

Setting _____ Date _____

Antecedent Events _____

Rumbling Stage

Student Behavior _____

_____

Teacher Interventions _____

_____

Rage Stage

Student Behavior _____

_____

Teacher Interventions _____

_____

Recovery Stage

Student Behavior _____

_____

Teacher Interventions _____

_____

Other Considerations

_____

_____

_____

Figure 3.5. Crisis report form.

Form. This analysis will help the team determine the effectiveness of the intervention. If successful, the plan may be continued with possible modifications and adaptations. If, on the other hand, the intervention is not as effective as hoped, it may be necessary to re-examine the function of the behavior, and develop and implement a new behavioral intervention plan and Student Crisis Plan Sheet (Figure 3.4).

Classroom Planning and Preparing for Tantrums, Rage, and Meltdowns

Adults must know how to handle the rage cycle in a child with AS and make plans accordingly. Such knowledge and preparation will help ensure that if a meltdown does occur, it can be addressed in a manner that will minimize student distress (Myles & Simpson, 1994a, 1994b, 1998, 1999).

The following is a series of steps that adults can take both as preventive measures and as actions during a rage episode.

Train Others to Respond to Rage

Adults who teach or live with the child with AS must be trained on what to do during the rage cycle. Written plans should identify adult roles, interventions to be used at each stage of the cycle, and methods to evaluate if the intervention was effective.

Practice for the Rage Cycle

Adults and children should be prepared for a meltdown. For example, both adults and children should know (a) where to go during times when students have meltdowns (e.g., what exits to use, where in the room to go); (b) who should be notified, how these contacts will occur, who will make the contacts, and so on; (c) what students not involved in the rage cycle should do during these occurrences; and (d) roles of other adults during the stages of the cycle.

Dress for Possible Meltdowns

Adults who support students who experience meltdowns should dress in a manner that will not interfere with their ability to respond appropriately to student needs. For example, wearing low-heeled shoes and loose-fitting garments, avoiding sharp jewelry and dangling earrings, and choosing short hair styles or wearing hair pulled back may increase the effectiveness of the adult responding to children and youth in the rage cycle.

Keep Items of Value Away from Children and Youth Who Experience Meltdowns

During the rage cycle, children may to attempt to destroy items important to their teachers. Such items should be removed from the classroom or kept away from students who may have tantrums, rage, or meltdowns.

Establish Trust and Rapport with Students

Children and youth with AS know when their teachers like and enjoy them. This relationship, while not eliminating tantrums, rage, and meltdowns, may reduce their occurrence. Therefore, it is imperative that adults let students know that they are liked and valued.

Teach Expectations

Adults must teach students rules and expectations. Many meltdowns occur because students do not know what they are supposed to do. Tai often began to "rumble" when his teacher would give three one-step directions because he could not process more than one direction at a time. Marga, a student who always followed the rules to a "t," became very upset when her teacher told the class that they needed to "buckle down and get to work." She could not figure out what she was supposed to buckle down and became very upset because she wanted to do what the teacher requested.

It is not enough that students are informed of expectations. The expectations must be taught so they are fully understood. Students with AS respond best to clearly structured settings wherein consistent positive and negative consequences exist for their behavior. Nevertheless, exceptions to this rule do exist, such as a student's cursing might be ignored during a meltdown, permitting the student to "save face."

Remain Calm

However difficult at first, the ability to remain calm can be learned with practice and experience. As discussed in Chapter 2, students are not available for learning during the rage cycle. Therefore, adults should acknowledge that their words are often not processed during this time. During the rage cycle, many adults talk to students to (a) let students know by their tone of voice that they are supporting the child and (b) keep themselves calm. Adults should *not* threaten. Rather, children should be calmly told rules and consequences, and what they need to do to end the cycle (e.g., "As soon as you are quietly seated, we can discuss this.").

Adults should also communicate that youth are permitted to be upset and angry in an appropriate manner (this is best *not* taught when the child is in the rage cycle). That is, in the teachable moment, adults should teach children and youth that everyone becomes upset and that it is okay to become angry, but it needs to be expressed in an appropriate way. Finally, adults should not argue with students but accept the fact that they will not win arguments with them once the rage cycle has started. Once a power struggle begins, the adult has already lost. It is much more productive to acknowledge students' feelings ("It's OK to be angry – sit down and we can talk about it."), ignore accusations, and assertively focus on steps needed to move the child to the recovery stage and ultimately to the teachable moment.

Finally, adults who work or live with children and youth with AS who experience meltdowns should be reminded that their job is to assist these individuals in acquiring skills and knowledge that will assist them in the future. That is, adults need to be active instructors – using the teachable moment to help students learn how to recognize that they are upset, how to express this behavior, and how to self-calm.

Schoolwide Measures to Meet the Needs of Children and Youth Who Exhibit Tantrums, Rage, and Meltdowns

Effectively serving children and youth with AS who experience rage in school requires adoption of schoolwide procedures such as those listed in the following that support the needs of these individuals and their families (Myles & Simpson, 1994a, 1994b, 1998, 1999). As underscored below, the major components of all these efforts include individualized services and effective communication.

Offer a Full Continuum of Services

Many students with AS who have meltdowns can succeed in general education classrooms. However, it is important that students are placed in a classroom that best meets their needs. That is, children and youth should have available to them a range of service options that meet their needs in the school and community.

Enhance Communication Across School, Home, and Community

To ensure that both student and family needs are met, and appropriate services are provided, efficient and effective communication lines must be established and maintained among school, home, and all agencies providing support to the child and family. To facilitate such efforts, a case manager should be identified to serve as the coordinator of school and community-based services for the child or youth with AS. This individual should be capable of developing and maintaining rapport and effectively communicating with staff across school and community-based agencies, as well as with parents and families.

Facilitate Parent and Family Involvement and Provide Maximum Family Support

Parents are equal partners with teachers and community-based agencies in providing support for the child or youth with AS. In fact, families are often key in providing long-term solutions to problems related to the cycle of tantrums, rage, and meltdowns. Thus, they should be directly involved in developing and implementing intervention programs.

Summary

Students with AS who exhibit meltdowns are most often served in general education settings. Thus, it is important that school-based personnel are able to plan and apply appropriate interventions for these students. Effective practice is based on careful observation and analysis of student behavior supported by classroom and schoolwide management systems with the input and involvement of parents and relevant community agencies.

Beyond these external systems and supports, the next chapter will examine specific strategies that promote internal control of one's behavior, including self-awareness, self-calming, and self-management.

CHAPTER 4

Strategies That Promote Self-Awareness, Self-Calming, and Self-Management

Children and youth with AS do not want to engage in rage behaviors. For most of them, the rage cycle is the only way they know of expressing stress, problems with coping, or a host of other emotions and situations to which they see no solution. Most want to become aware of their emotions and learn techniques for managing their behavior and calming themselves when faced with problems.

The best intervention to rage is prevention. Prevention occurs best as a multifaceted approach consisting of (a) instruction, (b) interpretation, (c) coaching, and (d) restructuring. However, as mentioned in Chapter 2, prevention strategies can only be taught effectively when the child or youth is not embroiled in the cycle of tantrums, rage, and meltdowns. As shown in Figure 4.1, teachable moments only occur when the child is calm, focused, and relaxed.

Instruction includes providing direct assistance by using a scope-and-sequence chart to identify skill areas in which the child may be deficient and providing direct instruction to teach those skills. *Interpretation* refers to the recognition that, no matter how well developed the skills of the person with AS are, situations will arise that he or she does not understand. As a result, someone in the environment must serve as an interpreter using a variety of techniques, including cartooning or social autopsies, to help clarify what is going on.

The third element in this multifaceted approach, *coaching*, recognizes that

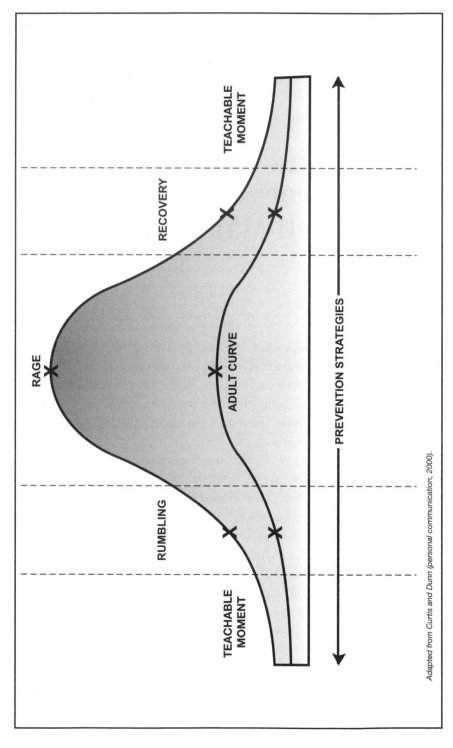

RUMBLING

RAGE

RECOVERY

TEACHABLE MOMENT

TEACHABLE MOMENT

ADULT CURVE

PREVENTION STRATEGIES

Adapted from Curtis and Dunn (personal communication, 2000).

Figure 4.1. Rage cycle.

while some children and youth know how to use a specific skill, they may not use it when appropriate. This may occur for a variety of reasons, including (a) difficulty generalizing the strategy so as to use it in the current environment or with a particular person, (b) experiencing a high level of stress that may have caused the child to temporarily "forget" the skills, and (c) forgetting the first step in using the strategy. Coaching provides the child with a "jump start" – a gentle nudge, a key word, or even script that can help the child use the skills. Finally, *restructuring*, the fourth component of effective programming, involves accommodations necessary due to the nature of AS. Ideally, the individual will learn over the years to restructure her environment or request necessary environmental modifications.

This chapter discusses interventions that have been found to be effective elements of a multifaceted approach. Many of the interventions fit into more than one of the four categories defined above. For example, social narratives can serve as both an instructional and an interpretive tool.

Instruction

Students with AS demonstrate many social and behavioral deficits and differences that require instruction to ensure they acquire skills that facilitate self-awareness, self-calming, and self-management – the major focus of this chapter. Most often, these students do not acquire many of the skills that we take for granted without a planned instructional sequence. In the following, under instruction we will discuss (a) scope and sequence, (b) direct instruction, (c) social narratives, (d) hidden curriculum, (e) acting lessons, (f) the Power Card Strategy, (g) self-esteem building, and (h) multimedia lessons.

Scope and Sequence

Because children and youth with AS evidence an uneven profile of social, behavioral, and communication skills, it is important to understand the sequence in which these skills develop. Without an understanding of scope and sequence, it is possible to overlook the fact that a child may be missing an important prerequisite skill that might make a more advanced skill become rote-based instead of a usable asset. For example, if a student does not understand that tone of voice communicates a message, teaching the more advanced skill of using a respectful tone of voice to teachers and other adults has little or no meaning. If the student learns by rote to use that tone of voice, she will probably not be able to generalize it.

Several scope and sequences exist that outline skills that specifically support self-awareness, self-calming, and self-management. For example, Howlin, Baron-Cohen, and Hadwin (1999) provide a sequence of development and instructional strategies for (a) the five levels of emotional understanding; (b) the five levels of informational state understanding, which includes perspective taking and predicting others' actions; and (c) the five levels of pretend play (see Table 4.1).

Table 4.1
An Overview of Skill Sequence and Instructional Strategies from "Teaching Children with Autism to Mind-Read: A Practical Guide" by Howlin, Baron-Cohen, & Hadwin (1999)

The Five Levels of Emotional Understanding
> Level 1: Recognizing facial expression from photographs
> Level 2: Recognizing emotion from schematic drawings
> Level 3: Identifying "situation-based" emotions
> Level 4: Identifying "desire-based" emotions
> Level 5: Identifying "belief-based" emotions

The Five Levels of Informational State Understanding
> Level 1: Simple visual perspective taking
> Level 2: Complex visual perspective taking
> Level 3: Understanding the principle that "seeing leads to knowing"
> Level 4: Predicting actions on the basis of a person's knowledge
> Level 5: Understanding false beliefs

The Five Levels of Pretend Play
> Level 1: Sensorimotor play
> Level 2: Emerging functional play
> Level 3: Established functional play
> Level 4: Emerging pretend play
> Level 5: Established pretend play

Howlin, P., Baron-Cohen, S., & Hadwin, J. (1999). *Teaching children with autism to mind-read: A practical guide.* London: John Wiley & Sons. Used with permission.

Howlin et al. also provide structured assessment in each of the areas, which includes establishing a baseline and teaching procedures that contain a strong visual component. For example, under teaching emotions, the authors provide instruction on how to identify "situation-based" emotions. Figure 4.2 includes a sample of general teaching principles related to identifying "situation-based" emotions and one of the many visual scenarios used to teach this concept.

General Teaching Principle

Whether correct or incorrect, the child is always provided with the general principle underlying the emotion.

When someone gives you something nice/you do something exciting (etc.), then you feel happy.

When something scary happens, you feel frightened and want to run away/hide.

When something nasty happens accidentally/people leave (etc.), then you feel sad.

When someone does something nasty to you on purpose (etc.), then you feel angry.

Figure 4.2. A sample of general teaching principles related to identifying "situation-based" emotions and a visual scenario used to teach this concept.

Frightening Situations

Teacher: Describe the picture to the child and ask the child either to say how the person in the story feels, or to point to one of the emotion faces below.

The big dog is chasing Dan down the road.

Emotion Question: How will Dan feel when the dog chases him?
Prompt–will he feel happy/sad/angry/afraid?

Justification Question: Why will he feel happy/sad/angry/afraid?

Figure 4.2. Continued

Howlin, P., Baron-Cohen, S., & Hadwin, J. (1999). *Teaching children with autism to mindread: A practical guide.* New York: John Wiley and Sons, Inc. Used with permission.

Another useful tool is offered by Duke, Nowicki, and Martin (1996), who designed a school-based scope and sequence to identify nonverbal language challenges in the areas of (a) paralanguage, (b) facial expression, (c) space and touch, (d) gestures and postures, (e) rhythm and time, (f) objectics, and (g) cross-channeling. For example, the facial expression unit contains lessons on (a) the resting face, (b) using eye contact, (c) horizontal zoning, (d) mimicking, (e) making faces, (f) varying intensity of expression, (g) varying the angle of expression, and (h) object imaging. Duke and colleagues also offer a curriculum and outline the features of a teaching and remediation program that are integrated into each of the nonverbal language areas, such as gestures, facial expressions, voice tone, as well as suggestions for how to facilitate the instructional process (see Table 4.2).

Table 4.2
Features of the Teaching and Remediation Program of "Teaching Your Child the Language of Social Success" by Duke, Nowlcki, & Martin (1996)

The purpose of teaching and remediation is to develop or improve skills. All of the activities in this book [*Teaching Your Child the Language of Social Success*] are designed to be:

- **systematic**: to teach in an organized way that makes sense to the pupil
- **ordered or graded**: to disclose increasingly complex information
- **cumulative**: to build and thoroughly explore each learning process before progressing to the next
- **multisensory**: to integrate visual, auditory, and tactile modalities
- **sympathetic**: to instill the confidence in each individual that a tutor understands his or her specific difficulties and wants to help

The following suggestions will facilitate the teaching and remediation process for all students, no matter their level of nonverbal communication skill:
- Maintain the child's interest.
- Set goals. Work on one area of improvement at a time.
- Give individual attention as frequently as possible. Encourage the student to ask many questions.
- Deliver new material more than once. Review and reinforcement are necessary.
- Help the student to relate new skills to past experience.
- Be positive and work on building the student's self-esteem.
- Allow children to learn any way they can, using any tools available.
- Practice.
- Practice.
- Practice!

Duke, M. P., Nowicki, S., & Martin, E. A. (1996). *Teaching your child the language of social success.* Atlanta, GA: Peachtree (pp. 32-33). Used with permission.

Another scope and sequence, from *Navigating the Social World: A Curriculum for Individuals with Asperger's Syndrome, High Functioning Autism, and Related Disabilities* (McAfee, 2002), contains a list of 20 social/emotional skills that address (a) recognizing and coping with one's own emotions, (b) communication and social skills, (c) abstract thinking skills, and (d) behavior issues. This scope and sequence (and accompanying lessons) seems particularly appropriate for girls with AS and related challenges. In fact, this excellent resource was developed by a mother, who is pediatrician, for her daughter. Table 4.3 provides a list of items on McAfee's scope and sequence.

Table 4.3

Navigating the Social World Social Skills Scope and Sequence

Section I: Recognizing and Coping with One's Own Emotions
1. Recognizing a Simple Emotion
2. Recognizing and Labeling More Emotions
3. Expressing Emotions
4. Recognizing Stress Signals and Causes/Effects of Stress
5. Self-Monitoring Stress Levels; Relaxation Strategies
6. Stress Prevention

Section II: Communication and Social Skills
7. Basic Conversational Responses
8. Recognizing and Interpreting Nonverbal and Contextual Clues in Other People
9. Greetings and Goodbyes
10. Initiating Conversations
11. Using Nonverbal Conversational Skills
12. Recognizing and Using Tone of Voice Clues
13. Conversational Manners
14. Making Introductions
15. Public vs. Private Information
16. Offering and Asking for Help
17. Giving and Receiving Compliments
18. Resolving Conflicts: Sharing Negative Feelings and Opinions

Section III: Abstract Thinking Skills
19. Figurative Speech

Section IV: Behavioral Issues
20. Compliance

Similarly, Baker (2003) offers a scope and sequence of 70 skills that teach communication and emotion management skills to children and adolescents with AS and related exceptionalities. Supported by many years of use in a clinical setting, Baker's scope and sequence is accompanied by an easy-to-use assessment measure that can be used by parents and educators. His assessment is unique in that it not only assesses whether the individual has a given skill, but also how often she uses it. Table 4.4 lists skills that appear on Baker's scope and sequence chart. Items checked on this menu of skills form the basics for a child's social skills program.

Table 4.4

Social Skills Menu

Student:_____ Date:_____

Person Completing Form:_____

(Check Items Relevant to Student)

Communication Skills

Conversational Skills
☐ 1. Maintaining Appropriate Physical Distance from Others ("Don't Be a Space Invader")
☐ 2. Listening Position
☐ 3. Tone of Voice
☐ 4. Greetings
☐ 5. How and When to Interrupt
☐ 6. Staying on Topic
☐ 7. Maintaining a Conversation
☐ 8. Taking Turns Talking
☐ 9. Starting a Conversation
☐ 10. Joining a Conversation
☐ 11. Ending a Conversation
☐ 12. Asking a Question When You Don't Understand
☐ 13. Saying "I Don't Know"
☐ 14. Introducing Yourself
☐ 15. Getting to Know Someone New
☐ 16. Introducing Topics of Interest to Others
☐ 17. Giving Background Information about What You Are Saying
☐ 18. Shifting Topics
☐ 19. Don't Talk Too Long
☐ 20. Sensitive Topics
☐ 21. Complimenting Others
☐ 22. Use Your H.E.A.D. (Happy Voice, Eye Contact, Alternating Turns, Distance)
☐ 23. T.G.I.F. (Timing, Greeting, Initial Question, Follow-Up Questions)

Table 4.4 (continued)

Cooperative Play Skills
- ☐ 24. Asking Someone to Play
- ☐ 25. Joining Others in Play
- ☐ 26. Compromising
- ☐ 27. Sharing
- ☐ 28. Taking Turns
- ☐ 29. Playing a Game
- ☐ 30. Dealing with Losing
- ☐ 31. Dealing with Winning
- ☐ 32. Ending a Play Activity

Friendship Management
- ☐ 33. Informal Versus Formal Behavior
- ☐ 34. Respecting Personal Boundaries
- ☐ 35. Facts Versus Opinions (Respecting Others' Opinions)
- ☐ 36. Sharing a Friend
- ☐ 37. Getting Attention in Positive Ways
- ☐ 38. Don't Be the "Rule Police"
- ☐ 39. Offering Help
- ☐ 40. When to Tell on Someone
- ☐ 41. Modesty
- ☐ 42. Asking Someone Out on a Date
- ☐ 43. Appropriate Touch
- ☐ 44. Dealing with Peer Pressure
- ☐ 45. Dealing with Rumors
- ☐ 46. Calling a Friend on the Telephone
- ☐ 47. Answering the Telephone

Emotion Management Skills

Self-Regulation
- ☐ 48. Recognizing Feelings
- ☐ 49. Feelings Thermometer
- ☐ 50. Keeping Calm
- ☐ 51. Problem Solving
- ☐ 52. Talking to Others When Upset
- ☐ 53. Dealing with Family Problems
- ☐ 54. Understanding Anger
- ☐ 55. Dealing with Making a Mistake
- ☐ 56. Trying When Work Is Hard
- ☐ 57. Trying Something New

Table 4.4 (continued)

Empathy
☐ 58. Showing Understanding for Others' Feelings: Preschool-Elementary
☐ 59. Showing Understanding for Others' Feelings: Preadolescent-Adulthood
☐ 60. Cheering up a Friend

Conflict Management
☐ 61. Asserting Yourself
☐ 62. Accepting No for an Answer
☐ 63. Dealing with Teasing – K-4th Grade
☐ 64. Dealing with Teasing – 5th Grade and Up
☐ 65. More Words to Deal with Teasing
☐ 66. Dealing with Being Left Out
☐ 67. Avoiding Being "Set Up"
☐ 68. Giving Criticism in a Positive Way
☐ 69. Accepting Criticism
☐ 70. Having a Respectful Attitude

Baker, J. (2003). *Social skills training for children and adolescents with Asperger Syndrome and social-communication problems.* Shawnee Mission, KS: Autism Asperger Publishing Company (pp. 23-25). Reprinted with permission.

Direct Instruction

Children with AS do not innately develop the social and behavioral skills necessary to be successful in school, home, and the community. As a result, teachers must provide an effective instructional sequence that facilitates skill acquisition, including (a) rationale, (b) presentation, (c) modeling, (d) verification, (e) evaluation, and (f) generalization. These steps may be followed whether using social skills lessons from traditional or nontraditional curricula as illustrated in the following pages.

Instructional Sequence

Rationale. In order to learn, many students with AS need to understand how or why concepts required for mastery are relevant. Thus, teachers must relate to the student (a) why the information is useful, (b) how the student can use the information, and (c) where the information fits with the knowledge the student already possesses. The rationale should include a visual task analysis that illustrates all the components of the lesson, including the amount of time to be spent on the lesson and which activities to complete.

Presentation. Once the rationale has been introduced, the teacher tells and shows the student the goals for the content and spells out exactly what the student has to learn. Then, using a direct instructional format, including both visual and auditory stimuli, the content is taught. Information is broken down into small increments and presented. This type of instruction is active, with the teacher presenting information, asking questions, and providing corrective feedback. In other words, direct instruction does *not* mean presenting a worksheet with a model and telling the student to follow the directions.

Modeling. During the modeling phase, the teacher first obtains the student's attention and then shows him what he is supposed to do. For example, the instructor may demonstrate how to participate in a cooperative group activity, how to use a specific paralanguage strategy, and how to complete a task or assignment correctly. This is particularly important as many students with AS know what *not* to do, but have no understanding of what is required of them.

Every direction is explicitly spelled out for the student, preferably using a visual aid. The teacher cannot infer that the student understands a concept or format just because it has been presented before. Anything that is merely implied by the teacher will likely not be understood by the student. Models should be presented frequently.

Verification. Throughout the lesson, the teacher closely monitors the student's emotional state. Because students with AS often have a flat, even seemingly negative affect, it is difficult to tell, for example, when they are stressed as a result of not comprehending specific content. The teacher must work with the student to understand how she communicates emotional distress and meet the student's needs as necessary through additional instruction, modeling, or individual work sessions. Failure to engage the student in this very important step can result in the student "tuning out" or, worse yet, having a rage attack.

Because of a propensity for tunnel vision and distraction/inattention, the student with AS must be actively engaged throughout the instructional process. For example, the student should be provided physical cues to attend to relevant stimuli and be asked frequent questions. Physical cues could take the form of the teacher using proximity control and tapping briefly on the student's desk using a prearranged signal, such as clearing the throat, placing a pencil on the student's desk, or placing a hand on the student's shoulder (see Chapter 2).

For the student with AS who requires a long processing time, the teacher might want to use a prearranged strategy so that the student knows when she will be asked a question. For example, the teacher might tell the student that she will only be asked a question when the teacher stands next to her. When using this strategy, the teacher initially asks the student questions to which the student already knows the answers. As the student becomes comfortable with the strategy and becomes more confident, the teacher can introduce questions that are more difficult. No one else in the class needs to know that the student and teacher have this agreement.

Evaluation. Following instruction, both the teacher and the student must evaluate skill acquisition. The teacher should employ a variety of methods to assess student understanding and use of the skill. Students, in turn, should self-evaluate their skill performance and set goals for generalization and skill maintenance.

Generalization. Programming for generalization must be a part of every lesson by arranging for opportunities for students to use newly acquired skills throughout the school day and in a variety of settings (e.g., physical education class, music). Teachers should also observe the student in less structured settings, such as lunch and recess, to determine whether the skill has truly been generalized. Finally, assistance from parents is invaluable to ensure generalization. Specifically, they can set up and/or observe home- and community-based events in which the students would be expected to use the skills.

Traditional Curricula

Several traditional curricula (that is, curricula designed for use by teachers and clinicians) may be used to provide direct instruction to children and youth with AS. Among the easiest to use is Baker's (2003) *Social Skills Training for Children and Adolescents with Asperger Syndrome and Social-Communication Problems*. The author has structured this curriculum so that educational professionals can plan a lesson in approximately 15 minutes. Each lesson includes a handout that summarizes the lessons and practice opportunities that can be given to parents, general education teachers, occupational therapists, and others who work and/or live with the individual with AS. Other curricula designed for individuals with Asperger Syndrome include the following.

- *Inside Out: What Makes Persons with Social Cognitive Disabilities Tick* by Michelle Garcia Winner (2000). Winner describes a number of cognitive processes that are challenging for individuals with AS and explores techniques that facilitate social thinking and related social development. A set of helpful worksheets accompanies each topic.

- *Let's Talk Emotions: Helping Children with Social Cognitive Deficits, Including AS, HFA, and NVLD, Learn to Understand and Express Empathy and Emotions* by Teresa Cardon (2004). This books offers a collection of easy-to-use activities on emotions for children ages 4-18. Children learn to identify and respond to their own feelings as well as the feelings of others.
- *Navigating the Social World: A Curriculum for Individuals with Asperger's Syndrome, High Functioning Autism, and Related Disorders* by Jeanette McAfee (2002). The author, a physician and parent of a child with AS, has created user-friendly programs to address social and emotional challenges.
- *Peer Play and the Autism Spectrum: The Art of Guiding Children's Socialization and Imagination* by Pamela Wolfberg (2003). This practical book teaches adults how to set up play groups with typical peers and children on the autism spectrum. Everything needed to set up and carry out play groups is included.
- *Relationship Development: Intervention with Children, Adolescents and Adults – Social Development Activities for Asperger Syndrome, Autism, PDD, and NLD* by Steven E. Gutstein and Rachelle K. Sheely (2002). The authors discuss strategies for establishing and maintaining social bonds. Over 150 easy-to-use exercises are presented. A special version for children ages 2 through 8 has also been developed, *Relationship Development Intervention with Young Children – Social Development Activities for Asperger Syndrome, Autism, PDD, and NLD.*
- *Super Skills: A Social Skills Group Program for Children with Asperger Syndrome, High-Functioning Autism and Related Challenges* by Judith Coucouvanis (2005). After a very helpful overview of the major issues related to social skills group training for children with autism spectrum disorders and other social cognitive deficits, this very practical resource presents a collection of 30 lessons grouped under four types of skills necessary for social success: fundamental skills, social initiation skills, getting along with others, and social response skills.
- *Thinking about YOU, Thinking about ME – Philosophy and Strategies to Further Develop Perspective Taking and Communicative Abilities for Persons with Social Cognitive Deficits* by Michelle Garcia Winner (2002). Winner discusses perspective taking and comprehending academic activities that have social implications. Practical ideas, strategies, worksheets, and ready-to-use IEP goals are included.

Nontraditional Curriculum

Social skills lessons can be supplemented with other materials that were not specifically designed for school use. The following is a brief list of books that may be used to teach social skills. Teachers and parents may want to preview the books before using them to ensure they teach the skills they want children and adolescents with AS to know.

- *The American Girl* series by Pleasant Company. Pleasant Company has published a series of books that are invaluable to girls of all ages. The books feature lifelike, attractive illustrations and use language that is informal, but informative. Books in the series include *The Care and Keeping of You: The Body Book for Girls* (Schaefer, 1998); *I Can Do Anything: Smart Cards for Strong Girls* (Kauchak, 2002); *Writing Smarts: A Girl's Guide to Writing Great Poetry, Stories, School Reports, and More!* (Madden, 2002); *The Feelings Book: The Care and Keeping of Your Emotions* (Madison, 2002); and *Staying Home Alone: A Girl's Guide to Feeling Safe and Having Fun* (Raymer, 2002).

- *As a Gentleman Would Say: Responses to Life's Important and Sometimes Awkward Situations* (Bridges & Curtis, 2001). Although this book is directed toward men (and male adolescents), it applies equally to women (and female adolescents). The book begins with 53 Things Every Well-Spoken Gentleman Knows, including how to listen, how to ask for favors, and understanding the meaning of "no." It also covers a diverse range of items related to lending and borrowing, dining out, meeting new people, and funeral behavior protocol.

- *Bringing up Parents: The Teenager's Handbook* (Packer, 1992). On the surface, this book appears to teach adolescents how to manipulate their parents to get what they want. In reality, Packer provides instruction on communicating clearly, being an active listener, taking responsibility for one's own actions, negotiating, and comprising. Topics include solving family problems, communicating effectively with parents, and coping with sibling issues.

- *How Rude! The Teenager's Guide to Good Manners, Proper Behavior, and Not Grossing People Out* (Packer, 1997). This book covers everything from getting along with peers to using "netiquette" (online etiquette). The book is fast-paced, entertaining, and written in teenager-friendly language.

- *How to Behave: A Guide to Modern Manners for the Socially Challenged* (Tiger, 2003). Designed for older adolescents and adults, this book covers travel by planes, trains, and automobiles; big-city living; leisure time; dating and love; and out on the town. It addresses issues that we often encounter, but with which few of us are prepared to deal, including lane blocking, tailgating, cutting others off, blocking, and merging when driving.
- *Life Lists for Teens* (Espeland, 2003). This book is a great resource for teens of all ages. It covers an extensive array of topics about life experiences, and how to get along, learn, and have fun.
- *A Little Book of Manners: Courtesy and Kindness for Young Ladies* (Barnes, 1998). This colorful book features Aunt Evelyn and Emilie, a pre-teen, who discuss telephone, mealtime, party, playtime and visiting manners, among other topics. The book is structured as a series of short vignettes that can be read by or to a child.
- *A Little Book of Manners for Boys* (Barnes & Barnes, 2000). In this book Coach Bob talks to boys about being good sports, taking care of things, eating, and other important issues. The book is written for boys between the ages of 6 and 12. Parents can read one item per day with/to a child and discuss it at the dinner table or at bedtime.

Social Narratives

Social narratives are brief written paragraphs that provide support and instruction for children and adolescents with AS by describing social cues and appropriate responses to social behavior and teaching new social skills. Written by educators or parents at the child's instructional level, and often using pictures or photographs to confirm the content, social narratives can promote self-awareness, self-calming, and self-management.

Minimal guidelines exist for creating social narratives other than to ensure that the content matches the student's needs and takes the student's perspective into account (Myles, Trautman, & Schelvan, 2004). Table 4.5 provides a set of guidelines that may be used to structure a social narrative for an individual with AS.

Two types of social narratives are commonly used: Social Stories™ (Gray, 1995, 2000; Gray & Gerand, 1993) and social scripts.

Table 4.5

Guidelines for Constructing Social Narratives

1. *Identify target behavior or problem situation.* A social behavior should be selected for change, preferably one whose improvement can result in (a) increased positive social interactions, (b) a safer environment, and/or (c) additional social learning opportunities. The behavior should be task-analyzed and based on the student's ability level.

2. *Define target behavior.* The individuals who plan and implement social narratives must clearly define the behavior on which data will be collected to ensure that everyone involved in the instructional process can reliably measure and interpret change. In addition, the behavior should be described in a way that the student can understand.

3. *Collect baseline data.* Baseline data should be collected over least three to five days. This will allow the educator and others to determine the trend of the behavior.

4. *Write the social narrative.* The narrative should be written in accordance with the student's comprehension skills, with vocabulary and print size individualized for each student. The stories should be written in the first or third person and either in the present (to describe a situation as it occurs) or the future tense (to anticipate an upcoming event).

5. *Display the narrative in a way that is commensurate with the student's functioning level.* For some students, one to three sentences per page is adequate. Each sentence allows the student to focus on and process a specific concept. Depending on the student's skill level, more than one sentence per page may result in an overload of information such that the student is not able to comprehend the information. Pictorial representations can enhance understanding of appropriate behavior, especially for students who lack reading skills. However, decisions about whether to use drawings, pictures, or icons in social narratives should be made on an individual basis.

6. *Read the social narrative to or with the student.* The teacher or student should read the social narrative as a consistent part of the student's daily schedule. Further, the student who is able to read independently may read the social narrative to peers so that all have a similar perspective of the targeted situation and corresponding appropriate behaviors.

Table 4.5 (continued)
Guidelines for Constructing Social Narratives

7. *Collect intervention data.* Data should be collected throughout the intervention process using the same procedures as for baseline data.

8. *Review findings.* If desired behavioral changes fail to occur after the social narrative intervention has been implemented for two weeks, the narrative and its implementation procedures should be reviewed. If program alterations are made, it is recommended that only one variable be changed at a time (e.g., only the content of the narrative, rather than simultaneously also changing the time the social narrative is read and the person who reads it). By changing one factor at a time, it is easier to determine the factor or factors that best facilitate individual learning.

9. *Program for maintenance and generalization.* After a behavior change has been established consistently, use of the social narrative may be faded. Fading may be accomplished by extending the time between readings or by placing additional responsibility on students for reading their own social narratives. Finally, students with sufficient independent skills may be assisted in identifying social goals for which they may develop their own related social narratives.

Social Stories™

Social Stories™ is an effective method of providing both guidance and directions for responding to various social situations that promote self-awareness, self-calming, and self-management (Gray, 2000; Gray & Gerand, 1993; Swaggart et al., 1995). A Social Story™ describes social situations specific to individuals and circumstances. For instance, Josh's grandmother was in the hospital and this 13-year-old with AS was understandably upset. He wanted to visit his grandmother in the hospital, but did not know the rules associated with such a visit.

A Social Story™ was developed to deal with this issue (see Table 4.6). It described the hospital, his grandmother's illness, why his grandmother was in the hospital, what he would see in his grandmother's hospital room, and what he should do during his visit. This Social Story™ and others like it involve structuring individual behavior and social responses by offering individualized and specific response cues. See Gray (2000) for instructions on how to write a Social Story™.

Table 4.6

Sample Social Story™

A Visit to the Hospital to See Grandma

by Virginia Cook

Grandma is sick in the hospital. I can visit her on Tuesday evenings after school. I should be able to visit her on most Tuesdays at the hospital. Grandma may look a little different because she is sick. She may have some tubes in her arms or in her nose and mouth. They are there to help make her better. Hospitals have many different kinds of machines to help people get better. Some of the machines make different sounds.

I will not use a loud voice inside the hospital. I will speak softly when I see Grandma, using the same voice I use in school or perhaps even a more quiet voice. She may not feel like talking when I visit or she may be asleep. I will only stay about 10 to 15 minutes because Grandma gets tired easily.

Doctors and nurses may come into the room to check on Grandma while I am visiting. If they come into Grandma's room, I will sit quietly until they are done visiting her.

When it is time to go, I may kiss Grandma softly and say goodbye. I can even tell her that I love her and miss her.

When I leave the hospital, I may use my normal voice again.

Social Scripts

Social scripts provide ready-to-use language for specific events. They may be structured as conversation starters, scripted responses, or cues to change topic (Kamps, Kravitz, & Ross, 2002). For instance, a child may practice a script that includes key questions that can help him begin a conversation with another child. For the child who has trouble spontaneously generating language, social scripts are effective because they help with language recall and assist the child in taking on another's perspective. Further, they minimize the stress students with AS often experience when approaching peers by reducing the probability of an unpredictable event occurring. When designing social scripts, care should be taken to include "child- or adolescent-friendly language." That is, common jargon should be incorporated as well as the informal language style used by peers.

Scripts do not work in every situation as they may make a child or adolescent sound over-rehearsed or robotic. The method is best used with model peers who understand the child, her characteristics, and the purpose of scripts. Table 4.7 provides an example of a social script for a fourth-grader with AS.

Table 4.7

Sample Social Script

Scenario

Jeremy frequently experienced difficulty when attempting to join his fourth-grade peers at recess. Without an invitation, Jeremy would barge into the group game, demand to be the center of attention, and take the role of what he considered to be the key player. That is, he wanted to be the pitcher in baseball, the quarterback in football, or the goalie in soccer. When the other children told Jeremy to wait his turn or not to play with them, Jeremy would wrestle the ball away from them and make them chase him. On several occasions, fights broke out.

A social script was developed to help Jeremy act appropriately when joining and participating in group games. Jeremy was coached in the use of the script, and in the early stages of its use he was accompanied by his teacher. Over time, the teacher faded his presence and Jeremy began to use the script independently.

Social Script

When I want to join a game at recess, I will stand near the children playing the game, but not on the field or in the way of the players. I will say, "Can I join in your game?" If the children say that I can, I will ask, "What position is open?" When I am in the game, I will follow the rules. If the children tell me not to play because the game has already started, or for some other reason, I will say, "OK, but I would like to play next time."

Hidden Curriculum

Every school and, indeed every classroom, has a hidden curriculum – the do's and don'ts that are not spelled out but that everyone somehow knows about (Bieber, 1994; Myles et al., 2004). For example, everyone knows that Mrs. Kristmann allows students to whisper in class as long as they get their work done, whereas Mrs. Rafik does not tolerate even the faintest level of noise in her class. Everyone knows that Mr. Johnson, the assistant principal, is a stickler for following the rules, so no one curses or even slouches in his presence. Everyone also knows that the really tough guys (the ones who like to beat up unsuspecting kids) hang out behind the slide, just out of teacher view. Everyone knows these things, that is, everyone except the student with AS.

Outside of school, the hidden curriculum is an even bigger issue. For example, what is the hidden curriculum for attending a nice restaurant?

1. You call ahead for reservations.
2. Upon arrival, you give the host/hostess your name and wait to be seated.
3. A waiter delivers a menu to you and may place a napkin in your lap.
4. And so on.

Somehow, a young person learns this hidden agenda. Perhaps he has been taught this curriculum from his grandmother; maybe he learned it from reading a book on etiquette. What if the student thinks this is appropriate restaurant behavior anywhere and attempts to generalize it to McDonald's? How long will he wait to be seated?

Consider the hidden curriculum associated with going to the library. When a teenage girl goes to the library with her father, she is there to check out a book. She talks quietly to her father, selects a book, checks it out, and leaves. This is one hidden curriculum for the library. However, there is another hidden curriculum for the library. When a teenage girl goes to the library with her friends, the curriculum is different. Chances are that she is not there only to check out a book and that she will not talk quietly, unless prompted to do so. The hidden curriculum of going to the library with friends is to socialize, have fun, and not be kicked out of the library.

Students with AS are at a disadvantage because they usually do not understand the hidden curriculum. They inadvertently break the rules associated with the hidden curriculum, thereby either getting in trouble with adults or becoming ostracized or hurt by peers. As a result, they require direct instruction on the hidden curriculum. They need to be taught that some middle-school students curse, but that no one curses in front of an adult, unless that adult is Ms. Gagnon, who tends to ignore such things. They need to know that only nerds wear tight-legged, high-water jeans to school. They need to know never to argue with a police officer, and so on.

Persons with AS also need to know (a) teacher expectations, (b) teacher-pleasing behaviors, (c) students to interact with and those to stay away from, and (d) behaviors that attract negative attention. Understanding the hidden curriculum can make a huge difference in the lives of students with AS – it can keep them out of detention or worse, and it can help them make friends. Temple Grandin developed her own set of rules, many of which are from the hidden curriculum, to guide her social interactions and behavior in society (see Table 4.8).

Who should teach the hidden curriculum? Many teachers voice concern at the prospect of having to teach certain elements of the culture ("I can't tell my students it is alright to curse in front of Ms. Gagnon."). Despite such reluctance, there are many hidden curriculum elements, such as how to interact with other students and adults at school, that teachers can comfortably teach and should teach as they would reading, writing, or social studies. There are other elements, such as understanding the rules associated with dating and developing intimate relationships, about which teachers should not provide instruction. In these areas, peer models can be enlisted. However, this should be done carefully. It is recommended that peers identify hidden curriculum items and then meet to discuss them with teachers and the student's parents. As a group they can decide when, how, and if to provide instruction. Table 4.9 provides a sample list of hidden curriculum items.

Table 4.8
Temple Grandin's Rule System to Guide
Her Social Interactions and Behavior

Temple Grandin developed this rule system to guide her social interactions and behavior

1. Really Bad Things – examples: murder, arson, stealing, lying in court under oath, injuring or hitting other people. All cultures have prohibitions against really bad things because an orderly, civilized society cannot function if people are robbing and killing each other.

2. Courtesy Rules – do not cut in on a line at the movie theater or airport, observe table manners, say thank you, and keep yourself clean. These things are important because they make the other people around you more comfortable. I don't like it when somebody else has sloppy table manners, so I try to have decent table manners. It annoys me if somebody cuts in front of me in a line, so I do not do this to other people.

3. Illegal But Not Bad – examples: slight speeding on the freeway and illegal parking. However, parking in a handicapped zone would be worse because it would violate the courtesy rules.

4. Sins of the System (SOS) – examples: smoking pot (and being thrown in jail for ten years) and sexual misbehavior. SOS's are things where the penalty is so severe that it defies all logic. Sometimes, the penalty for sexual misbehavior is worse than killing somebody. Rules governing sexual behavior are so emotionally based that I do not dare discuss the subject for fear of committing an SOS. An SOS in one society may be acceptable behavior in another, whereas rules 1, 2, 3 tend to be more uniform between different cultures.

I have never done a sin of the system ... People with autism have to learn that certain behaviors will not be tolerated – period. You will be fired no matter how good your work is if you commit an SOS at work. People with autism and Asperger's need to learn that if they want to keep a job, they must not commit an SOS ... The social knowledge required is just too complex.

Grandin, T. (1999, April). *Understanding people with autism: Developing a career makes life satisfying.* Paper presented at the MAAP Services, Incorporated, and Indiana Resource Center for Autism Conference, Indianapolis, IN. Used with permission of MAAP Services, Inc., PO Box 524, Crown Point, IN 46307; 219-662-1311, fax 219-662-0638 (chart@netnitco.net).

Table 4.9
Sample Hidden Curriculum Items

- Treat all authority figures with respect (e.g., police, firefighters). You would not address a police officer like you would your brother.

- Not all people you are unfamiliar with are strangers you cannot trust. You may not know your bus driver or your police officer, but these are people who help you.

- What may be acceptable at your house may not be acceptable at a friend's house. For example, although it is acceptable to put your feet up on the table at home, your friend's mom may be upset if you do that in their home.

- People do not always want to know the honest truth even when they ask. Your best friend does not want to hear that she looks fat in a new dress she just bought for the high school dance.

- Teachers do not have all the same rules. One teacher may allow chewing gum in the classroom, while another gives out fines for chewing gum.

- Teachers assume certain expectations for their students. For example, students are expected to greet the teachers, sit down when the bell rings, and listen quietly to announcements.

- When a teacher gives you a warning, it means that she wants a given behavior to stop and that most likely there will be a consequence if the behavior continues or occurs again.

- It is impolite to interrupt someone talking, unless it is an emergency.

- Acceptable slang that may be used with your peers (e.g., dawg, phat) may not be acceptable when interacting with adults.

- When the teacher is scolding another student, it is not the best time to ask the teacher a question.

- When a teacher tells another student to stop talking, it is not an appropriate time for you to start talking to your neighbor.

Myles, B. S., Trautman, M. L., & Schelvan, R. L. (2004). *The hidden curriculum: Practical solutions for understanding unstated rules in social situations.* Shawnee Mission, KS: Autism Asperger Publishing Company. Used with permission.

Acting Lessons

Many adults with AS and higher-functioning autism suggest that acting lessons are an effective means of teaching children and youth self-awareness, self-calming, and self-management. During acting lessons, children learn to express verbally and nonverbally their emotions in specific situations. They also learn to interpret others' emotions, feelings, and voices. Perhaps more important, in acting class participants engage in simulations and receive direct and immediate feedback from an instructor and peers regarding their performance.

One adult with AS, Margo, credits her success in expressing emotions and interpreting social situations to acting lessons. She acknowledges that her "real life" performances may be a bit stilted, but after taking acting classes she understands better how to act and react in a neurotypical world.

The Power Card Strategy

The Power Card Strategy is a visually based technique that uses a child's special interest to facilitate understanding of social situations, routines, and the meaning of language (Gagnon, 2001). This intervention contains two components: a script and a Power Card. A teacher, therapist, or parent writes a brief script at the child's comprehension level detailing the problem situation or target behavior, including a description of the behavior and a statement of how the child's special interest/hero has addressed the same social challenge, thereby generalizing the solution back to the child. The Power Card, the second component, the size of a business card or trading card, contains a picture of the special interest and a summary of the solution. Portable to promote generalization, the Power Card may be carried, or may be velcroed inside a book, notebook, or locker or placed on the corner of a child's desk (Gagnon, 2001). Figure 4.3 provides a sample script and Power Card used to help a student with AS.

Self-Esteem Building

The child or youth with AS may look different, act different, feel different, and, in some ways, is different from other people. The child often knows this, and loss of self-esteem is frequently the by-product. For adults, there is a high price to pay for a negative self-esteem. It has been documented that adults with AS have higher levels of depression, anxiety, suicide, and other affective disorders than the general population, which can partially be related to self-concept problems (Baron-Cohen, 1988; Bellini, 2004; Berthier, Santamaria, Encabo, & Tolosa, 1992; Ghaziuddin, 2002; Simblett & Wilson, 1993; Wing, 1981).

Jennifer

Jennifer is a second-grade student in a regular education classroom, who has a medical diagnosis of Asperger Syndrome. She has acquired many social skills, such as initiating a conversation and introducing visitors to the class, and she independently uses the school restroom. However, Jennifer consistently forgets to wash her hands after using the toilet.

Jennifer's teacher wrote the following scenario and POWER CARD featuring Angelica from Jennifer's favorite cartoon, *The Rugrats*, to remind her to wash her hands. An enlarged copy of Jennifer's POWER CARD was placed in the restroom to remind all the students of the proper steps to handwashing.

Angelica Says, "Wash Those Hands"
by Rachele M. Hill

Angelica knows how important it is to keep her hands clean. She does not want to catch any yucky germs from "those babies!" Germs can cause coughing, sneezing, and runny noses. Angelica definitely does not want to catch a cold! She washes her hands often and always after using the bathroom. She knows that washing her hands helps avoid catching a cold.

Angelica wants you to have clean hands, too. She wants you to remember to wash your hands often and every time after you go to the bathroom.

Angelica wants you to remember these three things:
1. Wash your hands after you go to the bathroom.
2. Always use soap.
3. Dry your hands completely.

Angelica can be very bossy, but she does have manners when it comes to having clean hands. Angelica says, "Please wash your hands!"

Figure 4.3. Use of a special interest to facilitate understanding of social situations, routines and the meaning of language.

Gagnon, E. (2001). *The Power Card strategy: Using special interests to motivate children and youth with Asperger Syndrome and autism.* Shawnee Mission, KS: Autism Asperger Publishing Company (p. 40). Reprinted with permission.

Educators and parents must work together to help children understand that they are more than the exceptionality. They are not AS. Yes, they have an exceptionality – but this is only one part of them. They have many other characteristics that must be pointed out and celebrated (Bieber, 1994). In fact, aspects other than the disorder should be the primary focus of a conversation about AS. The child should understand that all people are special. Everyone is able to do certain things well, while others are challenging. Throughout it is important to make sure that the exceptionality does not receive so much attention and focus that it becomes the major facet of a child's identity.

Ledgin (2002) has taken a different route to helping individuals with AS develop positive self-esteem. In his book, *Asperger's and Self-Esteem: Insight and Hope Through Famous Role Models*, he identifies 13 adults who seem to share some of the characteristics of AS. Among these are Charles Darwin, Orson Welles, Carl Sagan, Albert Einstein, and Marie Curie. Ledgin's message is that although individuals with AS have challenges, there is hope for the future, "Hope of success to which they may become entitled by their work and talent. Hope of their living a full, happy life that is everyone's entitlement. Hope of creating for us something unique and lasting, if that is the legacy they wish their special genius to represent for all eternity" (p. 40).

To foster understanding and acceptance of "different ways of being," Espin (2003) created a book for children 8 and up about a computer. She introduces readers to Alphie, a computer in a computer lab, who does not work like the other computers. For example, Alphie has been known to shut down without warning, eat disks, and freeze. Because people do not understand Alphie, they stay away from him. Luckily, a new computer manager is hired who takes the time to understand all of the computers, including Alphie. He spends some time programming Alphie (akin to teaching social skills) and then writes a set of directions that users can use with Alphie (teaching about individual differences). The book includes a guide that helps teachers and parents explain differences without applying labels.

Similarly, Faherty (2000) created a workbook for children and youth with AS to help them learn about themselves. Specifically, it facilitates self-awareness through a series of exercises, such as the one presented in Figure 4.4.

Another book, *What Is Asperger Syndrome, and How Will It Affect Me? A Guide for Young People* (Ives, 2001), also helps young people to understand their AS. While acknowledging that it is often difficult to explain AS to others and that people are generally not able to tell if somebody has AS just by looking at

Recognizing and Coping with One's Own Emotions

1. Recognizing a simple emotion
2. Redirecting negative thoughts to positive thoughts
3. Recognizing and labeling more emotions
4. Linking nonverbal clues to emotions
5. Expressing emotions
6. Quantifying emotions on a continuum
7. Stress I - Data collection, recognizing stress signals and causes and effects of stress
8. Stress II - Self-monitoring stress levels and relaxation strategies
9. Stress III - Stress prevention

Communication and Social Skills

1. Basic conversational responses
2. Recognizing and interpreting nonverbal and contextual clues in other people
3. Greetings and good-byes
4. Initiating conversations
5. Using nonverbal conversational skills
6. Making SENSE in conversations
7. Recognizing and using tone of voice clues
8. Conversational manners
9. Making introductions
10. Public vs. private
11. Offering and asking for help
12. Giving and receiving compliments
13. Resolving conflicts
14. Sharing negative feelings and opinions

Abstract Thinking Skills

1. Figurative speech

Figure 4.4. **Understanding Asperger Syndrome.**

Faherty, C. (2000). *What does it mean to me? A workbook explaining self-awareness and life lessons to the child or youth with high functioning autism or Asperger's.* Arlington, TX: Future Horizons (pp. vii-viii). Reprinted with permission.

them, the book sends a positive, yet realistic message. Ives concludes the book with these encouraging words to young people with AS,

It is important to remember that you are not alone. There are many people with Asperger syndrome. People with Asperger syndrome can go on to achieve a lot of things, including going to a university, getting a good job, living in their own house. You will always have Asperger syndrome although, as time goes on, you may get better at things you used to find really hard. ... Most importantly, remember that you are exactly the same person you always were, before you ever heard the words Asperger syndrome. Only now you have a way of understanding why you find some things tricky, and also can find ways of making life easier for yourself. (p. 20)

Finally, *This Is Asperger Syndrome* (Gagnon & Myles, 1999) fosters self-esteem for young children by presenting scenarios from a day in the life of a child with Asperger Syndrome. The whimsically illustrated book provides a depiction of how the child sees himself and others in social situations and discusses how others may have different perceptions, as illustrated in Figure 4.5.

I don't like the lunch lady. Today I asked her for more ice cream. She replied, "You need more ice cream about as much as you need a hole in your head." I got really scared because I thought she wanted to put a hole in my head with a drill. *This is Asperger Syndrome.*

Figure 4.5. **Fostering self-esteem.**

Gagnon, E., & Myles, B. S. (1999). *This Is Asperger Syndrome.* Shawnee Mission, KS: Autism Asperger Publishing Company (p. 10). Reprinted with permission.

A positive self-image is built, in part, by successful experiences. LaVoie (cited in Bieber, 1994) poignantly challenges teachers and parents to find the "island of competence" in the child, stress it, and celebrate it. Presenting multiple opportunities for the child to demonstrate his "island of competence" builds self-esteem. Several strategies to build self-esteem include:

1. Place the child with AS in the role as a helper or tutor.
2. Tell the child what he is doing right. Reframe negative language to positive language.
3. Find what the child does well and help her do more of it.
4. Compliment the child and teach him to compliment himself.

Multimedia Lessons

Since most children with AS are visual learners, interventions that use this modality are often especially successful. In addition to their visual format, using videotapes or DVDs offers several advantages when instructing individuals with AS. For example, (a) they show skills in a fluid format so that students can see them as a whole instead of as a set of discrete steps, (b) they are often motivating because of their pace and content, and (c) they allow for multiple viewings to ensure that students learn the skill that is targeted. Video modeling and video detective, discussed below, are two ways in which videotapes can be used.

Videos have been found to be effective for teaching emotional recognition. As mentioned below, vintage videotapes have been particularly successful. Finally, commercial software is available to teach emotional understanding and social skills.

Video Modeling

Using video self-modeling, individuals learn to interact with others by observing themselves on videotape engaging in an interaction. Although the use of video self-modeling has not been empirically validated with children and youth with AS, it has been used successfully with children with special needs exhibiting anxiety and/or depression (Dowrick & Raeburn, 1995; Kahn, Kehle, Jenson, & Clark, 1990) and autism (Buggey, Toombs, Gardener, & Cervetti, 1999; Charlop-Christy & Daneshvar, 2003; Charlop-Christy, Le, & Freeman, 2000).

One type of video self-modeling is known as *positive self-review.* Using this type, the child is taped when engaging in a behavior, and the video is used as a reminder for the child to engage in that behavior. Positive self-review is best employed when a child has developed a specific social skill, but is either (a) not using it at the appropriate level because it is newly acquired or (b) not maintaining it in the natural environment (Dowrick & Raeburn, 1995).

Another type of video self-modeling is called *feedforward*. This approach is used when a child has the component skills that comprise a social skill but has difficulty putting them together into a cohesive whole (Dowrick, 1999). For example, feedforward may be used when a child has learned individual skills but cannot put them together and use them in a real-life situation. In addition, it can assist students in transferring skills across environments. For example, JaeWook had learned all the steps to approach and talk with a peer during lunch, but when given the opportunity to use these skills, he would freeze after greeting a peer. To help him use the skills, his teacher videotaped JaeWook engaging in the steps he had learned to use and edited the tape so that it showed all the individual steps sequentially. When JaeWook saw the videotape, he was able to transfer the interaction skills to the lunchroom.

Video Detective

In another example of how to use videotapes, one mother teaches her son about nonverbal communication through *Saved by the Bell*, a television program about high school students. After she has introduced a concept, she plays the taped television show with the sound turned down and asks her son to predict the actors' nonverbal and verbal communication messages based on what he sees on the screen. Similarly, a middle school teacher routinely videotapes her class during planned simulations and regular activities and uses the tapes as instructional tools. For example, this allows students to see themselves giving mixed messages or using effective verbal strategies to communicate to others, and also to monitor their voice tone or proximity. The teacher also works with small groups of students to create scripts that the students act out on video. She plays the videotaped scripts and hosts two game show-type activities for her student contestants, "What's My Emotion?" and "Find the Conversation Flaw."

Care should be taken when selecting videos or television shows to be used as models for children with AS. Because of their highly visual format, shows may teach skills that were not intended. One young man learned social skills from *Walker Texas Ranger*, a show that features a law enforcement officer who often battles his opponents using karate. Unfortunately, he interpreted the message of the show as "If you don't get what you like or if someone is doing something bad, kick them. Then you will be a hero."

Vintage Videos

Vintage videos can also be excellent teaching tools. For example, Charlie Chaplin and Buster Keaton silent movies offer opportunities for individuals with AS to view facial expressions and link them with situations without having to navigate through spoken language. Similarly, the character Lucy Ricardo of the *I Love Lucy* videotapes offers exaggerated facial expressions that can also be helpful in teaching facial expressions.

Commercial Software

Authored by Simon Baron-Cohen and colleagues (University of Cambridge, 2003), the Mind Reading software program teaches human emotions to individuals who experience difficulty in this area. Students can see and hear 400 different emotions expressed in diverse people. In addition, the software package contains an emotions library, a learning center with lessons and quizzes, and a game zone that allows practice in a video-game type format.

Joining In! A Program for Teaching Social Skills by Linda Murdock and Guru Shabad Khalsa (2003) is a multi-video set that shows elementary-school peers modeling social skills. The instructors, a special educator and a speech-language pathologist, provide direct instruction on social skills and examples to viewers. The videotaped set targets conversation skills, school-based social skills, and interpersonal skills.

Interpretation

Social situations occur daily or even hourly that are taken for granted by the general population but make little or no sense to persons with AS, who often end up in trouble as a result. Even when the person with AS receives effective instruction about social and behavioral issues, situations will inevitably occur that require interpretation. Fortunately, a number of interpretative strategies can help turn seemingly random actions into meaningful interactions for individuals with AS. These include (a) behavior regulation; (b) sensory awareness; (c) cartooning; (d) social autopsies; and (e) the Situation, Options, Consequences, Choices, Strategies, Simulation (SOCCSS) strategy. We will discuss each option below.

Behavior Regulation

Behavior regulation includes the ability to read and self-monitor positive and negative reactions as well as to understand elements in the environment that may cause discomfort. As mentioned, children and youth with AS often have difficulty interpreting their emotions and social well-being. For example, research has shown that adolescents with AS are not reliable reporters of personal stress, anxiety, or depression. This is not because they are avoiding an uncomfortable situation or misleading themselves or others, but because they often cannot tell when they are feeling these emotions (Barnhill et al., 2000). In addition, many children and youth with AS have difficulty self-calming when they become upset (Dunn et al., 2002; Myles, Hagiwara, et al., 2004). Therefore, it is important to provide them with strategies that will help them understand their emotions and respond appropriately.

Two instructional strategies address this important topic. The first by McAfee (2002) works well with older students and educators who have substantive time to help students develop these skills. McAfee's visually based curriculum includes a strong component designed to assist students in decreasing stress by recognizing their emotions and redirecting themselves to a calming activity. Through the use of a Stress Tracking Chart, a Summary of Stress Signals Worksheet, and a Stress Thermometer, students with AS learn to:

- Identify and label their emotions using nonverbal and situational cues
- Assign appropriate values to different degrees of emotion, such as anger
- Redirect negative thoughts to positive thoughts
- Identify environmental stressors and common reactions to them
- Recognize the early signs of stress
- Select relaxation techniques that match their needs.

For examples of worksheets designed by McAfee for a student referred to as Scott W., see Figures 4.6, 4.7, and 4.8.

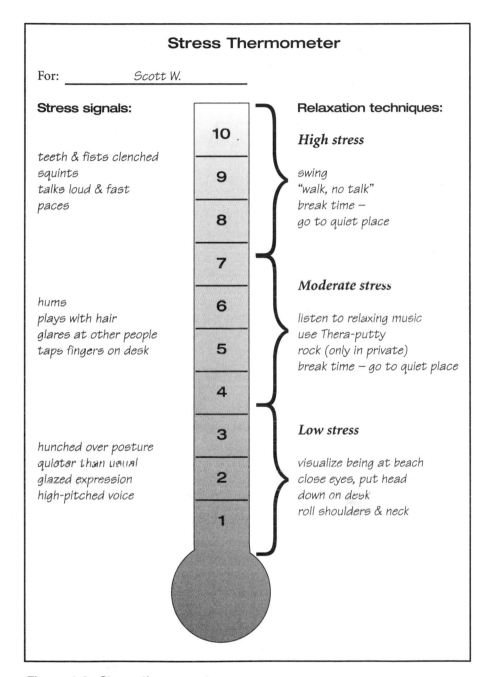

Stress Thermometer

For: _Scott W._

Stress signals:

teeth & fists clenched
squints
talks loud & fast
paces

hums
plays with hair
glares at other people
taps fingers on desk

hunched over posture
quieter than usual
glazed expression
high-pitched voice

10
9
8
7
6
5
4
3
2
1

Relaxation techniques:

High stress

swing
"walk, no talk"
break time –
go to quiet place

Moderate stress

listen to relaxing music
use Thera-putty
rock (only in private)
break time – go to quiet place

Low stress

visualize being at beach
close eyes, put head
down on desk
roll shoulders & neck

Figure 4.6. Stress thermometer.

McAfee, J. (2002). *Navigating the social world: A curriculum for individuals with Asperger's syndrome, high functioning autism and related disorders.* Arlington, TX: Future Horizons, Inc. (p. 47). Reprinted with permission.

STRESS TRACKING CHART

Home/School   Student: <u>Scott W.</u>

Date & Time	Precipitating event (trigger)	Underlying or "hidden" stressor(s) and related emotions	Body language, facial expressions & verbal cues (as observed)	Physical symptoms (by student report)	Stress level: Low, Moderate, High	Outcome
			Stress Signals			
4/1/00 9:30 am	Ian sat in Scott's usual chair during art class	Anxiety due to schedule changes that week	Playing with hair Humming	Not obtainable	Moderate	Shoved Ian • Sent to principal
4/2/00 10:10 am	Joe borrowed Scott's pencil and then lost it	Angry because he was teased on the school bus that morning	Jaws and teeth clenched Squinting	Muscles tense Increased heart rate	High	Shouted swear word Threw paperwork on floor • Sent to principal
4/5/00 2:30 pm	Scott didn't finish math problems before class ended	Frustrated, unable to concentrate due to noise from photocopy machine in next room	Humming Tapping on desk Playing with hair	Headache Stomachache	Moderate	Shouted at teacher that he "had to finish" • Points taken off math grade
4/6/00 1:30 pm	Bill accidentally bumped into Scott on playground at lunch	On playground for entire lunchtime. Difficulty joining in with other kids. Frustrated, lonely	Humming Glaring	Not obtainable	Moderate	Yelled at Bill and complained to playground aide • No further consequences

Figure 4.7. Stress tracking chart.

Date & Time	Precipitating event (trigger)	Underlying or "hidden" stressor(s) and related emotions	Stress Signals		Stress level: Low, Moderate, High	Outcome
			Body language facial expressions & verbal cues	Physical symptoms (by student report)		
4/7/00 10:05 am	Teacher gently corrected Scott's verbal answer in class	Some other students had giggled last period when Scott was reading report in front of class	Teeth & fists clenched Squinting Talking loud and fast	Face hot Heart pounding Breathing fast	High	Fumed out of room yelling, "I don't like any of you" • Discussion with teacher
4/8/00 3:15 pm	Joe slapped Scott on the back as a nice "hello" in hall	Group art project in afternoon	Hunched over	Headache Muscles tense Stomachache	Low	Scowled at other student • No further consequences
4/9/00 12:30 pm	Working on grammar assignment	Photocopy machine in next room	Glazed expression Quiet	Shoulder muscles tense Mild headache	Low	Unable to focus on work

Figure 4.7. Continued.

McAfee, J. (2002). *Navigating the social world: A curriculum for individuals with Asperger's syndrome, high functioning autism and related disorders.* Arlington, TX: Future Horizons, Inc. (p. 29). Reprinted with permission.

Summary of Stress Signals Student: _Scott W._			
	Low stress	**Moderate stress**	**High stress**
Verbal & nonverbal clues	Hunched-over posture Quiet, high-pitched voice	Humming Playing with hair	Teeth clenched Fists clenched Squinting
Body language, facial expressions & verbal clues (As observed by others. Data from Stress Tracking Charts)	Glazed expression	Glares Tapping fingers on desk	Talks loud & fast Pacing
Physical Symptoms (As reported by student. Data from Stress Tracking Charts)	Shoulder muscles tense Mild headache	Muscles tense generally Stomachache Headache	Muscles very tense Stomachache Sweaty palms Breathing very fast Increased heart rate Face hot

Figure 4.8. Summary of stress signals.

McAfee, J. (2002). *Navigating the social world: A curriculum for individuals with Asperger's syndrome, high functioning autism and related disorders.* Arlington, TX: Future Horizons, Inc. (p. 31). Reprinted with permission.

Buron and Curtis (2003) created the Incredible 5-Point Scale to help individuals with AS understand themselves and therefore be able to better regulate their behavior. The scale is unique in that it has a wide range of applications. For example, it can be used as an obsessional index, a stress scale, a meltdown monitor, and so on. Children and youth with AS learn to recognize the stages of their specific behavioral challenges and methods to self-calm at each level. The Incredible 5-Point Scale identifies in the child's own words (a) a term to describe her behavior at a 1, 2, etc.; (b) what the behavior feels like to her at each number; and (c) what the child, teacher, and/or parent can do to address the behavior at each level. Figures 4.9 and 4.10 provide two illustrations of how the Incredible 5-Point Scale may be used.

The Obsessional Index

Kevin is in the fifth grade. He has Asperger Syndrome and obsessive compulsive disorder. Kevin is obsessed with balls and will go to great lengths to find a ball and then throw it on top of the highest available ledge or roof. The ball-throwing obsession becomes a problem when he hurts others to get at a ball or when he runs through the school with a ball trying to find a high ledge. His anxiety over ball throwing is so intense that his thinking becomes illogical.

The following is Kevin's account of his ball obsession, which he reported to his teacher when she interviewed him as a part of a functional behavior assessment:

"I don't want to be obsessed with balls or balloons. It is a stupid obsession. I can't be the boss of anything. I want to be back to being a baby again. Maybe then I could start over. When I go to people's houses, I steal their balls, and that's embarrassing. No one in the neighborhood understands me. I hate obsessions. They make me mad. I really want to get rid of them but I can't. I can't do anything right. Every time I see a ball, I have to have it. I know right from wrong but this is just too hard."

The 5-point scale was designed to teach Kevin how to recognize his need for support in dealing with his obsessions before it was too late. On some days, he didn't even seem to think about balls; in fact, on those days his obsessive personality seemed to help him to stay focused on his work. On other days, he would think about balls but it didn't seem to bother him much. On those days, he was so relaxed that he could handle thoughts about balls.

Some days he just wanted to talk about his obsession with balls. If the adult with him told him not to talk about it, it often led to increased anxiety and acting-out behavior. Some days Kevin would come off the bus already talking rapidly about balls, types of balls, sizes of balls, and so on. We knew that on those days, he was going to need added support. This support often meant that Kevin did his work outside of the classroom to lower his anxiety about "blowing it" in front of the other kids.

Kevin had refused social stories in the past because he thought they were for "babies." Instead, we wrote him a memo to explain the new scale idea. Kevin loved the memo and kept it with him. He checked in with the special education teacher each morning to rate himself, and within a month he was accurately rating his anxiety about balls.

After we introduced the memo to him, there have only been a few days when Kevin had to work outside of the classroom for most of the day because his anxiety was high. Although he continues to have occasional rough days, he has not had to leave the classroom since we started the program.

Figure 4.9. The obsessional index.

M E M O

To: Kevin
Re: When Your Obsessions Get Too Big

Sometimes having obsessions can be a positive thing, because it means that your brain is capable of latching on to an idea and not letting go. This can be beneficial for great explorers, inventors and writers. BUT sometimes having obsessions can be very upsetting and frustrating.

This memo is to inform you that I understand that sometimes your obsessions get so big that you are not able to control them because of the severe level of anxiety they cause. It would be highly beneficial for you to learn to tell the difference between when your obsessions are too big to handle and when they are feeling more like positive obsessions. One way to do this is to do a "check-in" three times a day when you consider your obsessional index. The first step is to help me fill out the chart by rating your obsessional index on a 1-5 rating scale. Thank you for your cooperation.

Kari Dunn Buron

Figure 4.9. Continued.

Buron, K. D., & Curtis, M. (2003). *The incredible 5-point scale: Assisting students with autism spectrum disorders in understanding social interactions and controlling their emotions.* Shawnee Mission, KS: Autism Asperger Publishing Company (pp. 13-15). Reprinted with permission.

"I'm 6'2", Strong as an Ox – So Can You Tell Me Why I'm Trembling?"

David was referred to the self-contained high school program after being expelled from his home high school. He had broken several windows in the school cafeteria and the glass entrance/exit door nearest to the cafeteria. As a result, he had been to juvenile court and was placed on probation.

David identified his behavior as self-defense. "It was like my head was going to explode because of all the noise and confusion in the cafeteria. It's always confusing, and today there was a food fight. I had to do something to make it stop, I was afraid my head was going to explode."

The rating scale that follows does not rate David's level of anger, but his fear. David told us he feels afraid when he is "confused" so when developing this scale, we discussed things that we were afraid of, and David drew pictures to help him understand his own fear.

Understanding My Feelings

by David

Scared/Afraid

My word for this is:
trembling

This is how I look:

This is how my body feels:

This is what I do:
Hide.

This is what I say:
"I've got to get out of here!"

Things that David says make him "tremble":
"When I get confused."
"When it is loud and crowded."
"Catastrophes like tornadoes and earthquakes and war."

Figure 4.10. "Understanding my feelings."

Figure 4.10. Continued.

Buron, K. D., & Curtis, M. (2003). *The incredible 5-point scale: Assisting students with autism spectrum disorders in understanding social interactions and controlling their emotions emotional responses.* Shawnee Mission, KS: Autism Asperger Publishing Company (pp. 41-43). Reprinted with permission.

When My Autism Gets Too Big (Buron, 2003) is a structured yet flexible, child- and adult-friendly intervention that builds on the Incredible 5-Point Scale. This book addresses some of the biggest challenges experienced by many children and youth with AS – an inability to self-monitor stress, rapid escalation from worry to meltdowns, and difficulty knowing how to relax or return to a state of calmness. The author refers to this as "when autism gets too big." Used generically in this book, autism refers to the quick escalation to meltdowns experienced by individuals across the spectrum. This book is intended to help children with ASD understand that sometimes their autism does get too big and that they are not alone in this challenge (see Figure 4.11)

Figure 4.11. When my autism gets too big.

This might make me scream or even hit someone. This is a **5**. Now my autism is TOO BIG!

Figure 4.11. Continued.

Buron, K. D. (2003). *When my autism gets too big! A relaxation book for children with autism spectrum disorders.* Shawnee Mission, KS: Autism Asperger Publishing Company (pp. 13-14). Reprinted with permission.

Sensory Awareness

All of the information children receive from their environment comes through the sensory system. Taste, smell, sight, sound, touch, movement, the force of gravity, and body position are the basic sensory ingredients that enable all children and youth to listen, attend for a period of time, and be calm enough or awake enough to participate in learning experiences (Anderson & Emmons, 1996; Ayres, 1979; Myles, Cook, Miller, Rinner, & Robbins, 2000; Myles, Hagiwara, Dunn, Rinner, Reese, Huggins, & Becker, 2004; Williams & Shellenberger, 1996). Teachers and parents of children and youth with AS often assume that these children have an intact sensory system. This is not always the case; many have sensory integration dysfunction (Dunn et al., 2002). That is, they have neurological differences that do not allow them to process information or respond appropriately or in a timely manner.

Recognizing that sensory differences exist within individuals and acknowledging that children and youth, such as those with AS, can learn to self-regulate their sensory systems, Williams and Shellenberger (1996) developed a sensory integration program entitled *How Does Your Engine Run: A Leader's Guide to the Alert Program for Self-Regulation*. Designed for use by occupational therapists in conjunction with educators and parents, this program helps children to recognize their sensory needs. In addition, they learn to recognize their level of alertness or arousal and change it to best meet academic or social demands.

The Alert Program "uses the analogy of an automobile engine to introduce concepts of self-regulation to students. 'If your body is like a car engine, sometimes it runs on high, sometimes it runs on low, and sometimes it runs just right'" (Williams & Shellenberger, 1996, p. 2-1). Williams and Shellenberger provide instruction in 3 stages and 12 mile markers (see Table 4.10).

For example, through the Alert Program Susan has learned to recognize that her level of alertness is high as she enters school – she feels anxious and jittery. She also realizes that she needs a lower level of alertness to pay attention during her first class – math. From the curriculum, she has learned how to change her level of alertness. She knows that if she sits quietly for about 10 minutes and listens to some quiet music with headphones, she will be ready to attend to math instruction.

Table 4.10
3 Stages and 12 Mile Markers
of the Alert Program

STAGE ONE: Identifying Engine Speeds

1. Students learn the engine words.
2. Adults label their own engine levels.
3. Students develop awareness of the feel of their own engine speeds, using the adults' labels as their guides.
4. Students learn to identify and label levels for themselves.
5. Students label levels for themselves, outside therapy sessions.

STAGE TWO: Experimenting with Methods to Change Engine Speeds

6. Leaders introduce sensorimotor methods to change engine levels.
7. Leaders identify sensorimotor preferences and sensory hypersensitivities.
8. Students begin experimentation with choosing strategies.

STAGE THREE: Regulating Engine Speeds

9. Students choose strategies independently.
10. Student use strategies independently, outside therapy sessions.
11. Students learn to change engine levels when options are limited.
12. Students continue receiving support.

From: Williams, M.S., & Shellenberger, S. (1996). *How does your engine run? A leader's guide to the alert program for self-regulation.* Used with permission of TherapyWorks, Inc., 4901 Butte Place N.W., Albuquerque, NM 87120; 505-897-3478, fax 505-899-4071 (www.AlertProgram.com).

Cartooning

Visual symbols, such as schedules and cartooning, have been found to enhance the processing abilities of persons with AS and others on the autism spectrum and to enhance their understanding of the environment. Research has shown that visual support can serve as an effective means of teaching educational skills, functional living skills, and social skills (Kozleski, 1991; Krantz, MacDuff, & McClannahan, 1993; Kuttler, Myles, & Carlson, 1998; Rogers, & Myles, 2001).

One type of visual support is cartooning. The technique of cartooning, used as a generic term, has been implemented by speech/language pathologists for many years to enhance understanding in their clients, including to illustrate the meaning of idioms and to interpret social situations. Used in more specific ways, cartooning has played an integral role in several inter-vention techniques such as pragmaticism (Arwood, 1991), mind-reading (Hadwin Baron-Cohen, Howlin, & Hill, 1996; Howlin et al., 1999), and Comic Strip Conversations (Gray, 1995).

Comic Strip Conversations were introduced by Gray (1995) to illustrate and interpret social situations and provide support to "students who struggle to comprehend the quick exchange of information which occurs in a conversa-tion" (p. 2). Comic Strip Conversations promote social understanding by incor-porating simple figures and other symbols in a comic strip format. Speech, thought bubble symbols, and color are used to help the individual with AS see and analyze a conversation into its component parts. According to Attwood (1998), Comic Strip Conversations "allow the child to analyze and understand the range of messages and meanings that are a natural part of conversation and play. Many children with Asperger's Syndrome are confused and upset by teas-ing or sarcasm. The speech and thought bubble as well as choice of colors can illustrate the hidden messages" (p. 72). Educators or parents can draw a social situation to facilitate understanding or assist the student in doing her own illus-trations. You do not have to be a skillful artist to draw cartoons.

Tom, a 14-year-old with AS, was confused by conversations that girls were having with him. One in particular caused a meltdown. After Tom had regained self-control, his teacher asked him to relate the conversation that had distressed him while she cartooned what he said. Figure 4.12 shows Tom's conversation with a classmate, Mary, who had told him that he had a "cute butt." Tom, whose somewhat obsessive interest was legal issues, thought he was being sexually harassed by Mary and called her a "sexist pig." Mary retorted by calling him a jerk. In kind, Tom repeated the comment. Tom's teacher helped him to understand, through the use of a Comic Strip Conversation, that Mary was most likely trying to say that she liked Tom and that her feelings were hurt when she did not receive the expected response (an acknowledgment of her affection). The situation may have been further compounded when Mary was called a pig, particularly as she perceived her-self as having a weight problem and might have interpreted this remark as being directed toward that issue. Following the session with his teacher, Tom was able to understand Mary's hidden message and that he had probably hurt her feelings. He then made plans to apologize to Mary for having mis-understood her (Rogers & Myles, 1999).

Figure 4.12. Sample Comic Strip Conversation.

Social Autopsies

Social autopsies are particularly well suited to interpreting social and behavioral situations. Developed by LaVoie (cited in Bieber, 1994) to help students with severe learning and social problems understand social mistakes, a social skills autopsy is used to dissect social incidents so that individuals learn from their mistakes. When a social mistake occurs, the individual with AS meets with a teacher, counselor, or parent, and together, in a nonpunitive fashion, they identify the mistake and determine who was harmed by it. Then the student develops a plan to ensure that the error does not reoccur. Because of the visual strengths, problem-solving deficits, and language processing problems of the student with AS, social skills autopsies may be enhanced by using written words or phrases or pictorial representations to illustrate each of the stages. Lavoie overviewed the attributes and nonattributes of social autopsies, reiterating that it is a supportive, interpretive technique (see Table 4.11).

Table 4.11
Attributes and Nonattributes of Social Autopsies

A social autopsy is ...	A social autopsy is not ...
• Supportive, structured, constructive	• Punishment
• Solution-oriented	• Negative
• Opportunity for student participation	• Controlled and conducted by an adult
• A process for interpretation	• A "one-time" cure
• Conducted immediately after the social error	
• Conducted by any significant adult	
• Generally held in a one-on-one session	

Situation, Options, Consequences, Choices, Strategies, Simulation

The Situation, Options, Consequences, Choices, Strategies, Simulation (SOCCSS) strategy was developed to help students with social interaction problems put social and behavioral issues into a sequential form (Roosa, personal communication). The strategy helps students understand problem situations and lets them see that they have to make choices about a given situation and that each choice has a consequence. The SOCCSS strategy works as follows:

SITUATION: When a social problem arises, the teacher works with the student to identify the situation. Together they define the problem and state a goal. The stage occurs through discussion, writing, and drawings.

OPTIONS: Following identification of the situation, the student and teacher brainstorm several options for behavior. At this point, the teacher accepts all student responses and does not evaluate them. Typically, the options are listed in written or pictorial format. According to Spivak, Platt, and Shure (1976), this step is critical to problem-solving. The ability to generate multiple solutions diminishes student frustration, encourages students to see more than one perspective, and results in resiliency.

CONSEQUENCES: The student and teacher work together to evaluate each of the options generated. Kaplan and Carter (1995) suggest that each of the options be evaluated using the following two criteria: (a) Efficacy – Will the solution get me what I want? and (b) Feasibility – Will I be able to do it? Each of the consequences is labeled with an E for efficacy or F for feasibility. The teacher works as a facilitator, using pointed questions to help the student develop consequences for each option, without dictating consequence.

CHOICES: The student then prioritizes the options and consequences and selects a solution from the list of generated options. The student-selected option is the one that has the most desirable consequences.

STRATEGY: The student and adult work together to develop a plan of action. Although the adult may provide guidance by asking leading questions or making suggestions, the student should ultimately develop the plan so that he has ownership.

SIMULATION: The student is given an opportunity to turn the abstract strategy into something more concrete either through role-play, imagery, talking with a peer about the plan, or writing or typing the plan.

Figure 4.13 provides a worksheet that can be used to facilitate the SOCCSS process.

SOCCSS

Situation, Options, Consequences, Choices, Strategies, Simulation

Situation

Who _____   When _____

What _____   Why _____

_____

_____

Options	Consequences	Choice

Strategy – Plan of Action

Figure 4.13. SOCCSS.

Simulation	Select One
1. Find a quiet place, sit back and imagine how your *Situation* would work (or not work) based on the various *Options and Consequences*.	
2. Talk with a peer, staff, or other person about your plan of action.	
3. Write down on paper what may happen in your *Situation* based on your *Options and Consequences*.	
4. Practice your *Options* with one or more people using behavior rehearsal.	
5. _____	

Simulation Outcomes

Follow-Up

Figure 4.13. Continued.

Created by Myles, 1998, from the work of Roosa, J. B. (1995). *Men on the move: Competence and cooperation "Conflict resolution and beyond."* Kansas City, MO: Author.

Coaching

The third step in social support is coaching – helping children and youth with AS use the skills they have developed during social skills instruction and interpretation. Because individuals with AS often cognitively know skills but cannot apply them, this step is essential. A coach – parent, educator, mental health professional, or older child – upon observing the child in a social situation, can unobtrusively prompt the child to use a specific skill. Being a coach of a child or adolescent with AS requires that the individual understands the delicate balance between (a) providing support via coaching when needed and (b) allowing the student to independently use skills that he has mastered. Coaching should only be provided after the coach is certain that the child needs support to use a social skill. Coaching can take several forms: (a) feeding the language and (b) conversation starters.

Feeding the Language

Adults who are feeding the language (Collins, personal communication, 1999) to children with AS are verbally prompting the child toward a social activity. The prompt is conspicuous and may or may not contain a verbatim statement that the child is to say. That is, the adult must be extremely discreet when feeding the language. Only the child with AS knows that he is receiving social help.

Feeding the language may take many forms. An adult may:

- Point out another child who is alone and might want to interact socially. *"Marcus is standing over there by himself. I think that he might want someone to play with. Why don't you go over and talk to him."*
- Provide the child with AS a sentence or topic he can use in a social exchange.
  "Ask Libby if she has seen Sleepover. *If she has, you can say 'What did you like about the movie?' If she says that she hasn't seen the movie, say, 'What movies have you seen lately?'"*

Some individuals with AS become highly anxious when they attempt to enter into a conversation or other social interaction. Feeding the language provides a jump start – a verbatim sentence or phrase that the child can use to get started. Feeding the language might also include nonverbal cues. For example, an adult and student with AS might have a prearranged, discreet signal that cues the child to change topics, ask a question of a communicative partner, or move away from or toward someone, and so on. Signals may include touching an earlobe or clearing the throat. When selecting a signal, the adult must ensure that the signal is readily noticeable to the child but not to her peers. A second consideration is to ensure that the signal is not distracting. If the child looks intently for the signal, he may not be able to engage in a conversation with a peer. In this case, the signal becomes more important than the social interaction.

Conversation Starters

Beginning and maintaining a conversation requires a high degree of social skills and flexibility – two areas in which most children and youth with AS have challenges. Although they want to interact with peers, some do not know what to talk about. To remedy this situation a conversation starter card, the size of a business card or trading card, may be used. Such a card contains five or six different subjects that same-age peers would likely want to discuss, such as movies, musical groups, television programs, what someone did over the weekend (typically only good for Monday conversations), or fashion.

Topics are generally identified by listening to the conversations of peers in school hallways, at recess, or standing in line at a movie. It is important that conversation starter cards keep pace with current interests or activities. For example, it might be a good idea for the youth with AS whose peers often talk about music to bring up the rock group Weezer, who just released a new CD. However, it would be "uncool" to talk about a group whose album has been out for six months and is now considered old news. Topics must be gender sensitive as boys and girls find different topics interesting.

Restructuring

Restructuring or modifying the environment, the last topic to be discussed here, is a lifelong requirement for most persons with AS. Varying degrees of restructuring are necessary based on skill levels and learning styles. In most cases, as persons with AS become older, they are able to provide the modifications for themselves or request that they be implemented. Restructuring includes the use of visual supports, circle of friends, and environmental supports.

Visual Supports

As mentioned, students with AS benefit from information presented visually rather than auditorally because it is more concrete and allows for greater processing time. In the following, we will look at visual schedules, graphic organizers, timelines, and maps as visual supports serving different purposes.

Visual Schedules

Visual schedules take an abstract concept such as time and present it in a more concrete and manageable form. As such, they can yield multiple benefits for children and youth with AS, who often exhibit visual strengths. For example, visual schedules allow students to anticipate upcoming events and activities, develop an understanding of time, and facilitate the ability to predict change. Further, they can be utilized to stimulate communicative exchanges through a discussion of past, present, and future events; increase on-task behavior; facilitate transition between activities; and teach new skills.

Students may feel more comfortable when allowed to participate in preparing their own schedule. This should occur first thing in the morning. For example, students can assist in assembling their schedule, copying it, or adding their own personal touch in some other manner. This interactive time can also be used to review the daily routine, discuss changes, and reinforce rules.

Figure 4.14 provides samples of two visual schedules for students with AS. If the student is concerned about looking or acting different from others in the classroom, make sure that the visual schedule fits easily into the child's environment without attracting too much attention. Credit card-sized or bookmark formatted visual schedules provide structure, but can be used discreetly.

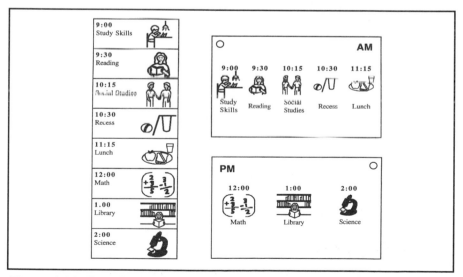

Figure 4.14. **Sample visual schedules.**

Schedules made with the Boardmaker™ and the Picture Communication Symbols. The Picture Communication Symbols © 1981-1999 are used with permission from the Mayer-Johnson Company, P.O. Box 1579, Solana Beach, CA 92075, 619-550-0084 (phone), 619-550-0449 (fax), and Mayerj@mayer-johnson.com (email).

Graphic Organizers

Graphic organizers, such as semantic maps, Venn diagrams, outlines, and compare/contrast charts, provide visual, holistic representations of facts and concepts and their relationship within an organized framework. That is, these strategies arrange key terms to show their relationship to each other, presenting abstract or implicit information in a concrete manner. They are particularly useful with content-area material such as social studies, science, and so on.

Graphic organizers can be used before, during, or after students read a selection, either as an advance organizer or as a measure of concept attainment following reading.

Graphic organizers often enhance the learning of students with AS because:

1. They are visual; this modality is often a strength for students.
2. They are static; they remain consistent and constant.
3. They allow for processing time; the student can reflect on the material at his own pace.
4. They are concrete and are more easily understood than a verbal-only presentation.

Figure 4.15 provides an example of a graphic organizer that may be effective for children and youth with AS.

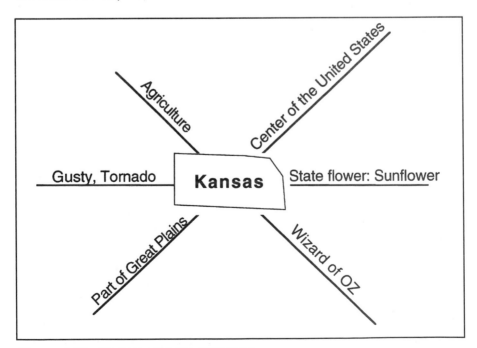

Figure 4.15. Sample graphic organizer.

Timelines

Timelines – something most of us use on a daily basis almost unconsciously – are another important form of visual support. Timelines break down assignments into their component parts and set deadlines for their completion. Because children and youth with AS often have difficulty with the concept of time, many think they can read a novel and write a 10-page paper the night before it is due. Others simply cannot get started when they are given a complex task; they do not know, without assistance, how to break it down into smaller pieces. As a result, they spend the entire time worrying about getting the assignment done without having a strategy to begin and/or complete the task.

Maps

Maps are extremely important for persons with AS, particularly at the middle school and high school levels. Often they cannot visualize where their locker is in reference to classes. For example, Josefa, a middle school student with AS, was on the verge of having to serve detention time for consistently being late to her classes. Following Josefa throughout her school day to determine the reason for her tardiness revealed that, very simply, Josefa was late to class because she went to her locker during each 10-minute passing time. For example, her second- and third-period classes were in the west wing of the building, but her locker was in the east wing. Instead of going to her locker after first period and gathering her books for the subsequent two periods, Josefa would race from the west wing to the east wing, and then back to the west wing. When given a map of the school showing her the most efficient ways to get from class to class and what books she should take with her each time she went to her locker, Josefa was able to change her pattern. Up until then, she had no idea that there was more than one way to get to any class, and she did not realize that it made more sense for her not to visit her locker between every class.

Circle of Friends

Helping students with AS develop friendships and support networks is integral to their school success. Because the desire for social interactions is typically high, involving the student with AS with peers is usually a strong motivator. In addition, it provides an excellent venue for students to practice social skills that they may have learned from adults in direct instruction situations. It is important to pair students with AS with socially astute and compliant buddies. Individuals who enjoy the way the person with AS looks at life are excellent candidates for a circle of friends. Those who participate in the circle must value the person with AS, not merely placate her and dictate her activities.

Establishing a "lunch bunch" is one way of using a circle of friends. In a lunch bunch three to four students eat together. The child with AS might bring a card of conversation starters or questions that she can use. The peers interact with her as a friend, helping her participate in lunch conversation. After eating, the lunch bunch might engage in a structured activity, such as a game, before returning to class.

Environmental Supports

Environmental supports can enhance student functioning both socially and academically. Children and youth with AS need an appropriate curriculum tailored to their often uneven skill profiles, including structured activities that allow them to show their skills. Students who appear to have learning disabilities or similar characteristics may be given strategy instruction to facilitate skill acquisition. For example, because of slow processing time, they may complete only the even-numbered items on a math worksheet. Because of motor difficulties, some students may be permitted to take a test verbally or to type a book report on the computer instead of writing it by hand. When notetaking is required, a peer may take notes using carbon paper and give the duplicate to the student with AS. The student who experiences problems with unaided recall may take a multiple-choice test instead of a short-answer or essay examination. The person who has trouble functioning successfully in cooperative groups is given a specific role in the group (i.e., timekeeper) or initially participates in peer tutoring sessions, or the individual with AS whose organizational skills make it difficult for homework to get home is given a homework hotline buddy who helps her to remember what assignments are due and when.

Adults working with children with AS should continually ask, "What can be done to make the environment more understandable for my student? How can I help him be more successful?" The ultimate goal is to help individuals with AS understand their exceptionality, complete with its strengths and challenges. From this understanding will come an awareness of the modifications the individual needs in order to be successful. Based on such understanding, the student with AS can be taught to be active in putting into place modifications that will help her show her skills in a positive way.

Summary

Helping students with AS increase and enhance self-awareness, self-calming, and self-management requires a multifaceted approach. This includes instruction related to social, behavior, and academic skills; help in interpreting the environment; coaching to help use existing skills; and restructuring to ensure that individual needs are met. With appropriate support through these means, individuals with AS will not need to resort to rage as the only option for communicating their wants and needs.

CHAPTER 5

Specifically for Parents

Amanda Lautenschlager – Mother of Benjamin and Ethan*

Many children and youth with AS experience the cycle of tantrums, rage, and melt-downs, leaving families to address this critical issue, often with little or no support. While we as professionals think we understand the impact of meltdowns on the family, we cannot truly know the havoc and heartache experienced by parents whose child is a victim of the rage cycle. In order to understand parents' experiences, we need an authentic voice.

Amanda Lautenschlager is one such voice. I have known Amanda via e-mail for approximately three years. She has e-mailed me with questions and sent some of the most innovative suggestions for addressing issues faced by families that I have heard. I asked her to co-write this chapter, adding her unique perspective to help readers understand family issues around the cycle of tantrums, rage, and meltdowns.

Brenda Smith Myles

The first time I read the first edition of *Difficult Moments*, I was completely overwhelmed. Finally, someone was able to describe what was happening in my family and provide some meaningful suggestions for how to cope.

---

* Ben is getting ready to graduate from high school and plans to attend college next year. Ethan will be transitioning to high school. Both boys have become fine young men. We are very proud of each of them. They continue to teach us about the specialized needs of our family (Amanda Lautenschlager).

My husband and I had witnessed the devastation of tantrums, rage, and meltdowns that had taken place in our family and could not imagine that anyone, anywhere could possibly help us. We felt isolated, ashamed, and out of control. Initially, the tantrums and meltdowns were sporadic. And for a long time, we thought most of our boys' problematic behaviors were typical of male siblings. In retrospect, we realize that we couldn't have been more wrong. The meltdowns gradually became more frequent. Over time the episodes became longer, increasingly dramatic, and much more emotionally draining. What was once a slammed door, a broken toy, or a ripped-up poster had escalated to a hole punched in the wall, a kicked-out windshield, and acts of self-abuse.

As the behaviors increased in severity and frequency, we began limiting our social interactions outside of our home. Even though we were not consciously aware of it at the time, it had become much easier to stay home than trying to go out to dinner or even visit friends. Social isolation just sort of crept up on us. Somehow we convinced ourselves that this was not abnormal behavior – after all, boys will be boys!

For our family, it took a major crisis to get our attention. The details of this crisis are not significant here. We had been in crisis for a long time but had not recognized the warning signs. We didn't know that our boys' behaviors were a form of communication. We didn't recognize how bad things had become and that they would only continue to spiral downward if nothing was done. What is important is the fact that we were able to overcome the difficult moments.

AS was virtually unheard of in our community. Fortunately, we received the help we needed although we had to fight for much of the support or create it ourselves. By spending countless hours on the Internet, reading every book we could get our hands on, attending conferences, and utilizing the services of our local community mental health center, we overcame the darkest of difficult moments.

I remember being angry that no one had ever told us of this book when it was first published, and at the same time feeling complete and utter relief that at least I had found it. Finally, we had an explanation that truly fit our situation. More important, we had strategies based on positive behavioral supports. We will always be grateful for this book and to Dr. Myles for sharing her many gifts with us. It is my hope that others will begin to find the answers they seek and that they too will come to know peace.

In this chapter, we will look at some ideas related to dealing with the rage cycle that are particularly useful for parents and families. Specifically, we emphasize the importance of family members agreeing on ways to deal with the sometimes challenging behaviors of AS, establishing routines to help everybody's life run more smoothly, communicating with schools and outside agencies, and parents taking care of themselves so they can ultimately take better care of their child with AS. We will also take a final look at the rage cycle.

Developing a Family Plan

It has been a long journey for us. We have overcome challenges that at one time seemed insurmountable. It hasn't been easy. At times we still struggle and probably always will, but things are different now. We support each other. By celebrating our strengths and sharing our weaknesses, we have become stronger individuals and a happier, more productive and cohesive family.

My husband, Scott, and I have learned that we must constantly re-evaluate ourselves, our children, and the things that are working well for us in addition to the things that present challenges. We have become experts on our own children with a special interest in meeting their needs. We have made sacrifices along the way. Scott works extended hours to support our family, and with his invaluable support I have been able to provide needs assessment, program development, management, and implementation in the areas of independent living, sensory, physical, occupational and language therapies, emotional and sensory regulation, social/leisure skills, cognitive and behavioral therapy, orientation and mobility, and self-determination. We have worked hard to develop comprehensive teams whose members have begun to take on the responsibilities that I previously assumed. We made these choices in order to empower our children – and to save. It has created financial strains, and at times been an overwhelming burden. Yet, we have been very fortunate.

The approach we have taken would be considered active by some standards. Certainly, it has taken a great deal of time and effort on our part. In addition to being full-time liaisons between our children and schools and other agencies, as parents, we have become social emotional interpreters, and hope our children will allow us to become their friends and partners. Partners share each other's burdens and find joy in mutual interests. As partners and friends we are able to view the world through the eyes of our children.

The more time we spend researching, implementing, reviewing and, most important, listening to and learning from our children, the more we have become aware of the scope of unmet needs that our kids live with. Having this knowledge and living in a world that has yet to make appropriate accommodations forces many of us to develop our skills as advocates. Effective advocates do more than protect and defend; they educate others. We are given a unique opportunity to teach others about AS and the supports and strategies that enhance the quality of our lives.

We start with our children's teachers and schools. As we are able, we expand this effort to our community recreation programs, public libraries, places of worship, and law enforcement agencies. By sharing information about our individual situations and supporting our cause with quick and easy-to-read materials, we increase our social, educational and occupational opportunities. Systems change is a huge task to undertake, but letters written to politicians and the heads of the departments of education, mental health, and developmental disabilities can be highly effective when we try to disengage from our role as parents and approach these people with accurate information that they may use to help make positive changes for the people they serve.

Special Tips for Multiparent Families

Multiparent families need to set aside time for the parents to come together to discuss the issues related to the behavioral challenges that affect every person in the home when a child with AS is involved. Families that have two or more parents experience stress due to the frustrations that arise when parents don't agree on the cause of behavior. This lends itself to even more difficulty when having to choose a strategy to deal with the behavior. By reaching an agreement, you will have more control over what happens in your own home. If your child spends time in more than one home, it may become necessary at some point to meet with the parents from the other home, but start out by focusing on the home in which you live.

In order to develop a workable and effective plan, both parents must agree to find common ground. Raising children is an emotional experience that challenges us to reflect on our own childhood and obstacles we had to overcome. In the process we become aware of different parenting styles that often lead to diverse decisions. Each parent has had different experiences and feelings that affect the decisions. As parents, all of us have undoubtedly experienced feelings of resentment towards our husband or wife at certain times. We don't always understand why our spouse does what he or she does. That is probably because we see things differently. Throughout, we must keep our ultimate goal in mind: the welfare of our child.

As part of developing a family plan, we will now look at the importance of agreeing on the causes of behavior and how to deal with behavior, guidelines for how to resolve conflicts (the LASTing word), and how to deal with siblings.

Agreement on the Causes of Problem Behaviors

Frequently, parents and other caregivers disagree on how much, if any, of the behavior exhibited by the child with AS is voluntary. One parent may be convinced that the behavior is under the child's control and, thus, require strict discipline to effect a change. The other parent, on the other hand, may see the behavior as part of the syndrome and insist that discipline not be used.

To make matters even more complicated, parents are often unaware of differences in their views. In some instances, one or both may become stronger in his or her beliefs to compensate for the other's behaviors. The result is arguments regarding how to parent the child. Often the child senses this difference and uses it to pit one parent against the other, thereby escalating already existing problems.

Unless the adults reach a joint understanding and acceptance of the cause of a given behavior and how to deal with it, the child will not learn new skills, and the caregivers will only become further polarized in their attempts to parent their child.

Many of the behaviors manifested by the child with AS are neurological in nature and are a part of the exceptionality. But how can you be sure? First, read books on AS; then attempt to identify similarities in behavior patterns delineated in those books and those of your child. Second, attend parent support group meetings. Listen to other parents. Are they experiencing similar problems? Third, talk to your child's teachers. Under similar circumstances and in similar environments, does the child engage in the behavior you read about?

If you find the same types of behaviors described in any of these three settings, it is most likely that at least some of the behaviors exhibited by your child are neurologically based. Caregivers within the family should discuss and then agree on which behaviors appear to be voluntary (i.e., chosen by the child) and which are a part of AS, and therefore involuntary. Then they can agree on which behaviors they will attempt to modify and the types of interventions to use.

The LASTing Word

Within any family, altercations between parents and children are inevitable. However, people who live in a family that has a member with AS often have more occasions for problem behavior. Often the rage cycle is exacerbated by the "last word." It seems that many children with AS need to have the "last word" in any discussion or exchange; many parents, however, believe that the last word should always rest with them. Thus, arguments go on interminably and often escalate to outbursts of rage.

To stop this cycle, consider the concept of the "LASTing word." In setting up this strategy, parents need to provide direction. One rule of thumb is to:

1. Say what you mean – mean what you say.
2. Say it only twice in a calm voice.
3. Verify the child's understanding. If the child processes information visually, the parent may need to choose her words carefully. Consider using icons or pictures to facilitate understanding.
4. Stop talking and take action; for example, by disengaging, implementing the previous steps, and so on.

Remember, it is not important to have the last word, but it imperative that parents have the LASTing word. In this way, children will learn to understand that they can count on parents to help set boundaries for them and enforce limitations.

Dealing with Siblings

When you have more than one child, it can be difficult to meet everyone's needs. Siblings of the child with AS must be able to express their feelings and talk about issues they are dealing with. Sometimes they just need someone to hang out with. Being a brother or sister of a child with AS has its ups and downs. It can be helpful to have someone to share both the pain and the joy with.

Some communities offer programs for kids who have a brother or sister with a disabling condition. Another way to support our children is by giving them one-on-one time with each parent or extended caregiver. This is a time when our kids should feel that they can tell us almost anything. Doing simple things that do not necessarily cost extra money such as going for a walk or doing the grocery shopping, yard work, or laundry becomes special when we focus on the needs of the child we are with. Setting a lunch date can be as simple as meeting at school and having lunch in the car. What is important here is the time we spend together, not the amount of money we spend together.

Designing a Daily Routine

As many children with AS do not have that inner clock that provides self-organization, it is important that parents create a daily plan. This plan will help the entire family in getting along and meeting the many and diverse requirements of their day. The plan must be fluid. Although it is built around a basic structure, it will require modifications as schedules change and as the child develops new skills.

It is critical that the plan be a family plan. Family members should work together to create the plan as well as decide when it should be reviewed and modified. Parents should also understand that there will be times when they will "blow it." That is, when, for some reason, they do not follow the plan. Part of the family plan should include how to handle these exceptions and how to get back into the routine once it has been broken.

A MOTHER'S PERSPECTIVE

When we started making changes in our home that includ ed implementing new strategies, we recognized that it would be a huge transition for all of us. We were excited about getting things underway and made a lot of changes in a short time. In order to ease the transition, I made lunch dates with the kids every week. When that couldn't happen for some reason, we set up individual shopping trips or play times.

At the suggestion of our case manager, once a week we also had family movie nights. When we were ready to work on more skills, we incorporated game nights into our plan. It reinforced the concept that we were all in this together. It was a great way for us to connect, and I think we all felt a stronger sense of belonging.

Morning Routine

It is common for children to have difficulty getting up in the morning. Often this problem is more marked for children and youth with AS, who seem to experience particular difficulty in adjusting to change (i.e., from sleep to awake; from recess to silent reading time). Young children who are awakened by their parents may require several wake-up calls and seem to do better with a gradual transition between sleep and awake.

As the child becomes older, she assumes more responsibility for getting up. Some families have found the two-alarm clock method to be helpful. A snooze alarm with music, set 30 minutes before actual get-up time, is placed near the child's bed. When it sounds, the child may turn off the snooze alarm and keep sleeping for the 10-minute intervals between the musical inter-ludes. A second alarm, which provides a loud and clamorous sound, sits across the room from the child's bed. It is set to go off at the actual get-up time. When this second alarm sounds, the child must go across the room to turn it off. An important part of the success of this structure is to teach the child to shower immediately after turning off the second alarm as this is most likely to prevent the child from going back to bed.

Even when the child is awake, she may not be in a complete state of alertness or arousal. Underarousal results in the child moping around. She exhibits low effort and motivation, lacks attention, and has difficulty focusing and processing information. Parents dealing with this type of child should use a calm voice, keep directions simple, and instruct in doing one thing at a time. Overarousal, on the other hand, results in the child being irritable and quick to anger. Such a child often has difficulty remembering things, and does not think clearly. Parents of an overaroused child should say as little as possible and refrain from assigning tasks that require clear thinking. They might want to consider the use of a cool zone (see Chapter 2) to help calm the child, as needed.

Dressing is another frequent problem in the morning routine. Alertness problems, which are common among children with AS, may cause inattention in selecting clothes. As a result, how the clothes look or feel sometimes becomes an issue. It is a good idea to have the child select clothes the night before to minimize any problems related to arousal level in the morning.

Further, many children with AS experience organizational difficulties and, consequently, have a difficult time collecting all the materials they need for school in the morning. Make sure the child learns to take proper care of homework, the backpack, lunch box, and other school materials. Many parents have posted near the door a visual schedule for their child with AS that shows all items needed for school. As a part of their bedtime ritual, children locate and pack all school materials.

Questions related to developing a morning strategy include:
1. How can a smooth transition between sleep and awake be structured?
2. How will the parent know if the child is under- or overaroused?
3. How will the parent react to the child when she is in each of these stages?
4. What steps are needed to help the child complete the morning routine?
5. Do visual supports or preparing the night before help the child complete the morning routine successfully?
6. Does eating a cereal bar or some other food on the way to the shower help if the child needs to eat first thing in the morning?

Homework

Distractibility, lack of organizational skills, and difficulty with handwriting are only three of the challenges many children and youth with AS experience that make homework completion problematic. Any or all of these characteristics combine to lengthen the time required to complete homework. When an excessive amount of time is required to complete homework, fatigue and the desire to watch television, for example, add to the potential for behavior problems.

Most schools recommend a certain amount of homework each evening. Parents and teachers should work together to ensure that the requirements for homework are not too intensive for the individual child. Children with AS should not be required to spend the majority of their evening hours doing homework. Further, some of the following strategies have helped make homework a less traumatic experiences for students with AS, as well as their families.

Distractibility can often be reduced by having an established routine that includes the same study hour and the same study place each day with all the necessary materials available. It is often best if the child is not in the vicinity of other playing children or the television. The child's attention span will dictate whether one long or several short segments should be structured for homework completion. Sometimes, the child's attention span can be expanded if an adult is present in the same room reading or engaging in an otherwise nonintrusive activity.

Because of their child's inherent lack of organizational skills, parents often have to help the child with AS get started on homework by providing a structure for work completion. Depending on the child's needs, such structure can be as simple as asking, "What must you do first," or as complex as creating a list of steps of what must be completed to finish a task or an assignment.

The issue of motor skills is also a consideration for many children with AS. For example, the child who has poor handwriting or who cannot complete a page without numerous erasures may need accommodations to avoid the strain and boredom that can result from having to write by hand. For example, the use of a computer or dictating to a parent or into a tape recorder may be options that help assist in homework completion.

The following issues should be addressed regarding homework completion:
1. What blocks the child from completing homework successfully?
2. What does the homework routine look like?
3. What interferes with homework completion? How can these interferences be minimized?

4. Should breaks be incorporated into the homework period? If so, how often should they occur, how long should they last, and what activities should be available to the child?
5. If organization is a problem, how can the parent help structure the child?
6. What accommodations should be made for homework completion?
7. Which caregiver can best help with which homework subjects?

A MOTHER'S PERSPECTIVE

Homework is a complicated issue. Sometimes school work is an area of strength for kids with AS, at other times it is highly challenging. Many of our kids exhibit splinter skills, meaning they excel in some areas and have difficulty in others.

As parents we have to ask ourselves what purpose the homework is serving. For example, if math presents challenges, it seems to make sense to look at how a particular math problem will benefit the child. Is it something he has to know in order to live successfully in the everyday world? Is it something he will need to know as an adult? Is there another way the problem could be taught?

In addition to these issues, we must be aware of the amount of homework that is assigned and the amount of time the child spends completing it. Some families find that a good portion of the evening is spent on homework. This is highly counterproductive for all involved.

If homework becomes an additional source of stress, is it really necessary? Are there steps we can take to relieve that stress? Are there alternate activities that will give our children an even more beneficial experience in the social world? Resolving these issues involves our children's teachers, and a team approach is warranted.

Chores

It is important that all family members have home-based responsibilities. Some children resist chores so much that it becomes easier for the parent to do them, but this is often not in the best developmental interest of the child. As a first step, parents should select one chore for the child to complete; initially, they may have to work along with the child to complete it. Pick a task that the child would like the most or, at least, resist the least. Even when the child can do more than one chore, the list should remain simple. Trying to remember several things at one time is difficult. A task list posted on the refrigerator is a good strategy to help students fulfill their chore responsibilities.

Parents cannot assume that the child knows how to do even the simplest chore. Consequently, the parent must model the chore, work alongside the child several times until she achieves independence, or make a visual display of the steps necessary to complete the chore. If the chore is not completed to the parent's satisfaction, fault finding is not a good way to improve performance. Neither is the temptation for the parent to redo the task. Instead, it is best for the parent and child to work through the chore together until it is done satisfactorily.

It is typically helpful to the child if a time frame for chore completion is established. Such a time frame should allow the child some flexibility, with completion tied to some natural event. For example, the child needs to complete the chore before watching television. This type of structure also serves as a natural consequence if the task is not completed.

Parents should ask themselves the following questions when assigning and monitoring chores:

1. What chores are reasonable for the child to complete?
2. What is the best way to teach the child to do the tasks?
3. What will time completion expectations look like?
4. What will happen if the chores are not completed properly?

A MOTHER'S PERSPECTIVE

When our kids are small, we help them become more independent by making simple charts that help them remember the things they have to do. As they grow, we gradually get rid of the charts and the rewards that went along with them. Older children are responsible for more complex duties and tasks. Sometimes they begin to struggle, and we may all find ourselves increasingly frustrated.

For some mysterious reason we expect our kids to know things that we have never thought, or taken the time, to teach them. Our kids have varied learning styles and needs. Some tasks require more support than others. Sometimes little or no help is necessary. At other times, every single step must be outlined, taught, and practiced repeatedly. In some instances, modeling or leading by example is necessary. At other times, a little bit of trouble-shooting is all that is required.

The key is to remember to remain flexible. Our kids' needs and levels of functioning change on a regular basis. We have to be able to change with them. As parents it is extremely beneficial for us to take a proactive approach and plan ahead. We must ask ourselves: Is my child capable of completing this task today? If so, what modifications must be implemented in advance so that my child will feel successful? If not, what alternate activities might be suitable?

Bedtime

Many children with AS have sleep disturbances that are manifested as (a) difficulties going to bed, (b) problems staying asleep or sleep walking, and (c) requiring more or less sleep than others.

One of the first questions to be resolved is whether bedtime should be set by a clock or the child's fatigue level. Most parents have some concept of a graduating bedtime based on the age of the child, but this does not always work with children and youth with AS.

Some parents allow their children to set their own bedtimes when they are tired enough to give in to sleep. Other parents select a bedtime for their child. If the child is not ready to sleep at the predetermined time, she is allowed to complete quiet activities in bed (e.g., coloring, reading, listening to calming music). Whatever strategy is selected, enough sleep time must be structured so that the child can get up in the morning and prepare for the day with few problems.

Transitioning to bedtime is often a problem for children and youth with AS. Many require an advance warning. Sometimes a calming activity such as playing a quiet game with a parent or reading a book are good options to precede bedtime. Some parents use this transition time as a quiet one-on-one time with their child to simply enjoy each other's company.

If the child consistently resists sleep, it is important to investigate the underlying causes. These may include, but are not limited to: (a) bedtime fears, (b) obsessive thoughts that will not stop, (c) bedtime compulsions, (d) wanting to be with parents, (e) wanting to have the same bedtime as older siblings, or (f) reaction to medication. Each situation is dealt with differently. For example, if bedtime compulsions are a problem, reading or listening to music may help. If medication is a problem, a consultation with the child's physician may lead to changing the dosage or the time the child takes the medication.

The following should be considered relative to bedtime:

1. What should set bedtime: child fatigue or a predetermined time?
2. How can the child be transitioned into bedtime?
3. What is the bedtime routine?
4. If the child resists bedtime, what is the cause? What can be done to minimize this resistance?

Sleep Problems

When our children don't sleep, parents are not able to rest either. The resulting exhaustion makes it difficult to be effective at anything we attempt. All sleep experts seem to agree on the fundamental behavioral strategies that are supposed to enhance sleep. Specifically, the National Institute of Health reports that a growing body of scientific evidence shows that inadequate sleep results in tiredness, irritability, frustration, and difficulties with focusing attention and controlling impulses and emotions.

In children, inadequate sleep may lead to excessive daytime sleepiness, interfering with a child's ability to learn in school and perform well in other activities. Many children with chronic sleep deprivation may not seem sleepy and may even appear to be overactive. Chronic sleep loss in these children may be overlooked or erroneously attributed to hyperactivity or behavior disorders.

To help alleviate bedtime problems:

1. Set a regular time for bed each night and stick to it.
2. Establish a relaxing bedtime routine, such as giving your child a warm bath or reading a story.
3. Make after-dinner playtime a relaxing time. Too much activity close to bedtime can keep children awake.
4. Avoid feeding children big meals close to bedtime.
5. Avoid giving children anything with caffeine less than six hours before bedtime.
6. Set the bedroom temperature so that it's comfortable – not too warm and not too cold.
7. Make sure the bedroom is dark. If necessary, use a small nightlight.
8. Keep the noise level low.
   (http://www.nhlbi.nih.gov/health/public/sleep/starslp/about.htm)

Some parents find themselves spending countless hours tracking their children's sleep patterns in order to determine the cause of the disturbance. One parent spent an entire month charting his child's every waking hour in search of some type of pattern. Finally, he came to the conclusion that they had to acknowl-edge that when their child woke up, she needed to eat. In order to address the problem, they taught their child to eat something that did not require a great deal of preparation and after eating to go immediately back to bed. They were careful to teach that this meant going back to sleep, and not to turn on every light in the house as the child made her way back and forth to the kitchen.

When we have exhausted all of the traditional options, it sometimes becomes necessary to investigate alternatives. For example, some families rely on homeopathic remedies such as Melatonin or herbal teas. Other families consult clinics that specialize in pediatric sleep disorders. Some families have had great success by undergoing sleep studies and utilizing specialized machines, such as the C-Pap.

One child who went to one of these clinics did not register sleep apnea. However, the clinicians acknowledged that the boy never reached the state of REM (rapid eye movement) sleep. Given the boy's history, the clinicians agreed to try a C-Pap machine. The boy was able to reach the REM state the very first night that the machine was used and finally got a good night's sleep. Yet other families put a television set in the child's bedroom tuned to programs that are not highly engaging to the child but mildly entertaining. When children are able to relax in this fashion, the sleep process may be facilitated.

A MOTHER'S PERSPECTIVE

When dealing with sleep issues, keeping our homes and fam-ilies safe must be our first priority. After safety has been established, it becomes necessary to consider the needs of the primary breadwinner and primary caregiver. The bottom line is that you have to get adequate sleep, if you want to help your family. A sense of balance must be found in order for everyone to be able to face the challenges that lie ahead.

Home-School Communication

Developing a positive partnership with teachers and school personnel can be overwhelming. Many of us – teachers, parents, and students alike – have had at least one negative experience that was enough to make us flinch at the idea of a partnership and the word "positive" ... forget about it! Some school districts embrace new learning opportunities and empower their teachers to meet the diverse needs of the students they serve. Others make it difficult for teachers to provide accommodations – even those that are federally mandated. In some situations communication between parents and teachers is nonexistent.

Whatever the reason, there will come a time when we as parents must make contact with our child's school. Perhaps the child is having meltdowns that cannot be traced to the home or other community environments. In preparing for such situations, it is critical that we analyze the approach we will take. We do not want to unwittingly create a situation that will result in even more challenges. It can be helpful to remind ourselves that the main goal is to start a dialogue that will be conducive to creative problem solving with regard to meeting the needs of our children. In many instances it becomes necessary for parents to teach teachers about their family situation, the things that seem to make life easier for them, or the things that produce difficult moments.

A MOTHER'S PERSPECTIVE

Sometimes teachers can be more receptive to understanding the individual needs of our kids if we are able to present them with short, easy-to-read items that have been published by leaders in the field of AS or have been empirically validated (see Table 5.1). Copies of articles or parts of a book that you have found especially helpful may be helpful to your child's teacher as well. Providing documentation of the strategies you are implementing often helps to give parents' comments greater validity in the eyes of professionals. If you are working with a case manager in the mental health field, consider inviting him or her to become part of your child's team. An effective case manager can be an additional support when discussing personal issues.

Keeping in mind that we all have different learning styles, and make decisions based on our own experiences, it may be helpful to set up regularly scheduled meetings with school staff. Team meetings should allow team members to come together to share information, create strategic planning opportunities, engage in creative problem-solving, and celebrate the accomplishments of our children and the team members who support them. Team meetings should be structured in a manner that allows for positive results.

Table 5.1
Useful Sources of Information About
Asperger Syndrome

Books

Attwood, T. (1998). *Asperger's Syndrome: A guide for parents and professionals.* London: Jessica Kingsley.

Baker, J. (2003). *Social skills training for children and adolescents with Asperger Syndrome and social-communication problems.* Shawnee Mission, KS: Autism Asperger Publishing Company.

Barnhill, G. P. (2002). *Right address ... wrong planet: Children with Asperger Syndrome becoming adults.* Shawnee Mission, KS: Autism Asperger Publishing Company.

Bleach, F. (2001). *Everybody is different: A book for young people who have brothers or sisters with autism.* Shawnee Mission, KS: Autism Asperger Publishing Company.

Buron, K. D. (2003). *When my autism gets too big! A relaxation book for children with autism spectrum disorders.* Shawnee Mission, KS: Autism Asperger Publishing Company.

Buron, K. D., & Curtis, M. (2003). *The Incredible 5-point scale. Assisting students with autism spectrum disorders in understanding social interactions and controlling their emotional responses.* Shawnee Mission, KS: Autism Asperger Publishing Company.

Clark, J. (2005). *Jackson whole Wyoming* (children's book). Shawnee Mission, KS: Autism Asperger Publishing Company.

Cohen, J. (2002). *The Asperger parent: How to raise a child with Asperger Syndrome and maintain your sense of humor.* Shawnee Mission, KS: Autism Asperger Publishing Company.

Gagnon, E., & Myles, B. S. (1999). *This is Asperger Syndrome* (a children's book). Shawnee Mission, KS: Autism Asperger Publishing Company.

Haddon, M. (2002). *The curious incident of the dog in the night-time* (novel). London: Jonathan Cape.

Moon, E. (2003). *The speed of dark* (novel). New York: Ballantine Books.

Moore, S. T. (2002). *Asperger Syndrome and the elementary school experience: Practical solutions for academic and social difficulties.* Shawnee Mission, KS: Autism Asperger Publishing Company.

Myles, B. S. (Ed.). Special issue: The face of Asperger Syndrome. *Intervention in School and Clinic, 36*(5). Austin, TX: Pro-Ed.

Myles, B. S., & Adreon, D. (2001). *Asperger Syndrome and adolescence: Practical solutions for school success.* Shawnee Mission, KS: Autism Asperger Publishing Company.

Myles, B. S., Cook, K. T., Miller, N. E., Rinner, L., & Robbins, L. A. (2000). *Asperger Syndrome and sensory issues: Practical solutions for making sense of the world.* Shawnee Mission, KS: Autism Asperger Publishing Company.

Myles, B. S., Trautman, M. L., & Schelvan, R. L. (2004). *The hidden curriculum: Practical solutions for understanding unstated rules in social situations.* Shawnee Mission, KS: Autism Asperger Publishing Company.

Table 5.1 Continued

Myles, H. M. (2003). *Practical solutions to everyday challenges for children with Asperger Syndrome.* Shawnee Mission, KS: Autism Asperger Publishing Company.
Savner, J. L., & Myles, B.S. (2000). *Making visual supports work in the home and community: Strategies for individuals with autism and Asperger Syndrome.* Shawnee Mission, KS: Autism Asperger Publishing Company.
Shore, S. (2003). *Beyond the wall: Experiences in autism and Asperger Syndrome* (2nd ed.). Shawnee Mission, KS: Autism Asperger Publishing Company.
Shore, S. (2004). *Ask and tell: Advocacy and disclosure for people on the autism spectrum.* Shawnee Mission, KS: Autism Asperger Publishing Company.

Other Resources

Maap Services, Inc.
http://www.maapservices.org/

Maap Services, Inc.
P.O. Box 524
Crown Point, IN 46307
Phone: 219-662-1311

Autism Society of America (ASA)
http://www.autism-society.org

Autism Society of America
7910 Woodmont Avenue, Suite 300
Bethesda, MD 20814-3067
Phone: 301.657.0881 or 1.800.3AUTISM

Geneva Centre for Autism
www.autism.net

Geneva Centre for Autism
112 Merton Street
Toronto, Ontario
Canada M4S 2Z8
Phone: (416) 322-7877 or 1-866-Geneva-9 (toll free in Canada)

Online Asperger Syndrome Information and Support (OASIS)
http://www.udel.edu/bkirby/asperger/

Outside Agencies

Families that include children with challenging behaviors and social emotional needs are subject to increased stress and anxiety. Additional issues may involve obsessive-compulsive disorder, attention deficit disorder, depression, concerns for the future, finances, and being able to find adequate child care. Sometimes we need to seek outside assistance. For example, it may be necessary to contact state protection and advocacy agencies, state mental health agencies, or agencies for individuals with developmental disabilities.

Availability of programs and services depends upon where you live. Further, your income and level of need will determine if community mental health services are available at a free or reduced rate. A case manager is usually assigned to help sort through all of the issues families are faced with. Effective case managers are aware of available services and supports, and should be able to help ensure that needed services are in place. If you are not satisfied, you have the right to and should consider interviewing more than one case manager to find a good match.

When seeking help from outside agencies, keep the following points in mind:

- Services vary from location to location.
- The way mental health services are delivered changes with every person/ institution you contact. For example, one provider may see her role as that of supportive listener. Another might consider himself your personal savior and set about trying to "fix" whatever he deems broken. Still others will understand that what is needed is support. These are the people who are able to acknowledge that they must assimilate themselves to your family's needs. This is the type of provider who will acknowledge that there are many ways to approach a situation and that interventions must be suitable to your individual family. Providers should be willing to read the current information available regarding AS and help you to utilize proactive strategies as you become willing and able.
- Before setting up appointments for family members, make arrangements to meet with the therapist alone to make sure he or she is a good match for the family and the particular issues to be addressed. It will save lot of time and frustration in the long run, as it helps to weed out therapists who do not appear to be an appropriate match for your family.
- Every counselor/therapist has different views regarding family structure. Ask questions to get a clear understanding of how they operate. If you are not comfortable with the answers, or the tone of the conversation, find another source of assistance.

A MOTHER'S PERSPECTIVE

Many services utilized by individuals with developmental disabilities, for example, are not available to individuals with AS because their average-to-above intelligence makes them ineligible for programs they could otherwise benefit from. Searching for adequate mental health services can be time consuming and frustrating. Once you have found someone who appears to be a good choice for your family, be aware that in many instances traditional interventions such as sitting in an office and going over emotions or behaviors are generally not as productive as getting out into the community and actually practicing proactive strategies.

Perhaps interpersonal relationships within the family will be a good place to start. Your child may need help understanding his role within the family. Other family members, in turn, may need help understanding the variety of roles and supports that are needed and how they can help.

Many providers need accurate information about AS. After numerous non-effective attempts, our family was blessed to finally receive services that met our needs. In fact, we would not be where we are today if we had not received the assistance of service providers who were willing to learn along with us.

Taking Care of Yourself

Support Groups

As parents who live with daily challenges that many others do not encounter, some of us enjoy being part of a group who can relate to the unique issues that we are faced with. Every support group functions differently. Some groups are set up for sharing, others are designed for strategic planning, for obtaining services, and for learning new information. Some have a specific focus while others cover many areas of need.

If you cannot quite find what you are looking for, try sharing these feelings with the group. You might find that other members feel the same way. Another option to consider is joining a Web-based group. For those of us who live in smaller communities, the Internet can be an amazing source of information, proactive strategies, fellowship, and respite. If you do not have your own computer, check with your local library. Most libraries offer free access to the Internet. In addition, they usually have staff who are able to help you get started.

The level of support that others can offer sometimes depends on how proactive you can or want to be. Through no fault of their own, some people do not understand our situation. It is up to us to decide how much we want to share with them. Social isolation can be difficult to overcome. Information is available on how it can affect our children. Less information is available on the toll it takes on the rest of the family.

Again, we have to take a step back and realize that our lives are very different from those of a lot of other families. There is no way for others to fully understand our differences unless we help them. Helping others find ways to help us requires an additional effort on our part, including an extra dose of patience and positive support. We know that our children are beautiful, interesting, joyous, loving people who face challenges in their day-to-day activities. By helping our extended families, friends, and neighbors learn about all of the great qualities our children possess, we open the doors of communication and help to increase the positive environmental/community supports that our kids desperately need. And by sharing information related to strategic ways to meet our children's needs, we empower others to offer help.

Respite

All parents need time away from their children – time to have an identity outside of being parents. They need time to go to a movie, go to the library, or just relax without their child being their primary concern. The need to get away once in a while is particularly strong for parents of children with special needs.

For parents, respite offers the opportunity to relax and re-energize, which is in the best interest of the entire family. For the child with AS, respite care offers time with a trained babysitter or care provider, an opportunity to have new experiences and generalize skills across people and environments.

Some states provide funding for respite care and/or flexible family support funds. More information on these programs can be obtained from your state Division of Developmental Disabilities. Some families and/or children are eligible for Supplemental Security Income (SSI) benefits. SSI, a federal provided by the Social Security Administration, is based on financial need and determination of disability. In many cases the level of disabling condition must be determined.

The Rage Cycle

Although the rage cycle was discussed at length in Chapter 2, there are some specific considerations for parents whose children experience tantrums, rage, and meltdowns. Each child's rage cycle has a pattern – the rumbling stage occurs first, followed by the meltdown. Some of the prominent characteristics at each stage are:

1. During the rumbling stage, the child exhibits a pattern of behaviors that build. These behaviors may include biting nails or lips, lowering the voice, tensing muscles, tapping the foot, grimacing, or other indication of general discontent.
2. There is typically a sudden onset of the rage.
3. Quite often the behavior appears to be unprovoked; however, there is a cause.
4. The rage appears grossly out of proportion to the situation.
5. The child gets no pleasure from the behavior, is often remorseful afterwards, and wants the episodes to stop.
6. During the rage cycle, the child is not thinking rationally. Thus, reasoning with the child at this stage does not work.

Often the best thing to do is to attempt to implement some of the techniques described in Chapter 2 if the behavior is in the rumbling stage (e.g., antiseptic bouncing; "just walk and don't talk"). If the child is in the rumbling stage or early stages of the meltdown, assisting the child to a cool zone or home base is one of the best options. In the cool zone, the child can relax so that she can once again have control. The cool zone is not a disciplinary procedure; it is an area in the house that contains stress-reducing activities that help the child refocus.

Parents also need to plan a strategy for a graceful exit for the child when they see escalation building. The child may not have sufficient emotional maturity to read his own internal clues and will therefore rely on the parent to cue that the rage cycle has begun. By carefully observing the child, the pattern of signals exhibited during the rumbling stage can be identified. If, by agreement, the parent and child have developed a nonintrusive sign that the safe room is needed, the child can be signaled.

Sometimes during a meltdown, the child will cling to the parent. It is important that parents disengage from the child in a calm and unemotional manner. The parent may need to make comments such as, "I know this is hard for you," "No matter what, I love you," or "It is time to work through this." Remember, the less said, the better. The child is not thinking rationally and parents' immediate goal should be to get out of the cycle.

The following questions should be asked relative to the rage cycle:

1. What behaviors does the child exhibit during the rumbling stage?
2. What strategies will the parent use during this stage?
3. What behaviors does the child exhibit during the rage stage?
4. What strategies will the parent use during this stage?
5. Where will the cool zone be located in the house?
6. How will the child be directed there?
8. What strategies can the parent use to disengage from the child who is in the rage cycle?

A MOTHER'S PERSPECTIVE

When we have attained a basic understanding of the challenges our children face, we have laid the foundation that is needed to understand the difficult moments that are a direct result of the challenges associated with AS. We don't know exactly what a typical day is like for our kids, but we can try to imagine. Think about your own day and how many different situations you encounter from the minute you wake up until you go to bed. How much anxiety and stress are you living with?

Now, imagine a world where no one seems to understand you, what is important to you, or why you do the things you do. Not only that, consider the fact that you would be struggling to understand what others mean when they speak and why they do the things they do. Add to that possible sensory issues, depression, ADHD, and difficulty regulating your emotions. Would you be happy? How long would you be able to contain your dissatisfaction? How would you get your needs met?

Interventions

When trying to develop interventions for dealing with your child's rage cycle, start out by listing the physical cues your child exhibits during the rumbling stage. If you are not sure, refer to the examples in Chapter 2. In the future you will be able to identify the signs that are unique to your child. As your child grows, keep in mind that some of the cues may change. So be constantly observant and vigilant.

Now list the interventions that you feel you can try when you recognize the rumbling stage. For ideas, review the suggestions given throughout this book. Follow the same procedure for the rage stage and the recovery stage. This list will serve as a quick reference at times when options are needed. If you're not sure about the patterns your child has developed, you may need to make some observations. This may require devoting a great deal of attention to things for a while. On the other hand, it may fall into place rather quickly. Either way, this will be a learning experience for everyone.

Once you have chosen the interventions you will start with, take the time to discuss with your spouse (if single, discuss with any other family member or caregiver who will be involved) exactly how each strategy will be utilized with every person who is going to implement it.

Once everybody involved is familiar with the strategies you have chosen and knows what to do, share/practice them with your child when he or she is not in or anywhere near a state of crisis. Start out with the method that seems most likely to work the best. You always have the option of trying a different approach the next time.

Remember:
- Every child is different.
- Each stage of the rage cycle is different.
- Strategies change from cycle to cycle.
- Strategic plans must include options.

Along the way things may level off, get worse, then better – then worse again. Plan for it. Plan on taking a step back and re-assessing the path you're on by asking some very basic questions such as: Are the goals appropriate? Are they functional? Are we happy? When things start to get better, do we want to incorporate additional strategies? When things hit a rough patch, what approach will we take? Think about your short- and long-term goals for your child, yourself, and your family. There are a lot of options. Seek help if necessary.

Summary

Creating effective environmental, emotional, community, and social supports for the people we care about are short- and long-term goals that each of us must consider. As families emerge stronger, happier, and healthier after working their way through difficult moments, they are challenged to develop strategies that will effect positive change. Each of us must answer this call as we are able.

At different points along the path toward our newly discovered freedom, we may have encountered feelings that we are not particularly fond of. For example, it is not uncommon to feel a sense of resentment for the things we may have missed out on. Perhaps we have felt victimized, that we were dealt an unfair hand in the game of life. Many emotions come up along the way.

Fortunately, as human beings we have the power of choice. By choosing to face these feelings and accept them as a part of our existence, we become empowered to choose our reactions to the feelings. Overcoming difficult moments reminds us of the greatness of which we are capable, the opportunities we have been afforded, and the awesome nature of our existence. Many of the things that we were once unable to do become possible and even ordinary. For some it can become a day worthy of celebration when we are able to do things such as stopping off at the grocery store or going out to a restaurant. Family vacations that may have seemed out of reach are not only possible, but enjoyable for everyone.

There are many issues that must be addressed head-on to help children and youth with AS function at home and enjoy their parents and siblings. Parents must provide a structure that is compatible with their own needs and the needs of other family members to help the person with AS function appropriately and happily within the family. It takes a lot effort and can be exhausting at times, but the rewards are numerous for the entire family.

References

Adams, J. I. (1997). *Autism-P.D.D.: More creative ideas from age eight to early adulthood.* Toronto, Ontario: Adams Publications.

Albert, L. (1989). *A teacher's guide to cooperative discipline: How to manage your classroom and promote self-esteem.* Circle Pines, MN: American Guidance Service.

American Psychological Association. (2000). *Diagnostic and statistical manual of mental disorders* (4th ed.; text revision). Washington, DC: Author.

Anderson, E., & Emmons, P. (1996). *Unlocking the mysteries of sensory dysfunction: A resource for anyone who works with or lives with a child with sensory issues.* Arlington, TX: Future Horizons.

Arwood, E. L. (1991). *Semantic and pragmatic language disorders* (2nd ed.). Denver, CO: Aspen.

Asperger, H. (1944). Die 'autistichen psychopathen' im kindersalter. *Archiv fur Psychiatrie und Nervenkrankheiten, 117,* 76-136.

Attwood, T. (1998). *Asperger's Syndrome: A guide for parents and professionals.* London: Jessica Kingsley.

Autism Asperger Resource Center. (1997). *Assessing the setting demands in the classroom.* Kansas City, KS: Author.

Ayres, J. (1979). *Sensory integration and the child.* Los Angeles: Western Psychological Services.

Baker, J. E. (2003). *Social skills training for children and adolescents with Asperger Syndrome and social communication problems.* Shawnee Mission, KS: Autism Asperger Publishing Company.

Barnes, E. (1998). *A little book of manners: Courtesy & kindness for young ladies.* Eugene, OR: Harvest House Publishers.

Barnes, B., & Barnes, E. (2000). *A little book of manners for boys.* Eugene, OR: Harvest House Publishers.

Barnhill, G. P., Hagiwara, T., Myles, B. S., Simpson, R. L., Brick, M. L., & Griswold, D. E. (2000). Parent, teacher, and self-report of problem and adaptive behaviors in children and adolescents with Asperger Syndrome. *Diagnostique, 25,* 147-167.

Baron-Cohen, S. (1988). An assessment of violence in a young man with Asperger's Syndrome. *Journal of Child Psychology and Psychiatry, 29,* 351-360.

Baron-Cohen, S., Jolliffe, T., Mortimore, C., & Robertson, M. (1997). Another advanced test of theory of mind: Evidence from very high functioning adults with autism or Asperger Syndrome. *Journal of Child Psychology and Psychiatry, 38,* 813-822.

Beck, M. (1985). Understanding and managing the acting-out child. *The Pointer, 29*(2), 27-29.

Bellini, S. (2004). Social skill deficits and anxiety in high-functioning adolescents with autism spectrum disorders. *Focus on Autism and Other Developmental Disabilities, 19,* 78-86.

Berthier, M., Santamaria, J., Encabo, H., & Tolosa, E. (1992). Recurrent hypersomnia in two adolescent males with Asperger's Syndrome. *Journal of the American Academy of Child and Adolescent Psychiatry, 31,* 735-738.

Bieber, J. (Producer). (1994). *Learning disabilities and social skills with Richard LaVoie: Last one picked ... first one picked on.* Washington, DC: Public Broadcasting Service.

Blackshaw, A. J., Kinderman, P., Hare, D. J., & Hatton, C. (2001). Theory of mind, causal attribution, and paranoia in Asperger Syndrome. *Autism, 5,* 147-163.

Bridges, J., & Curtis, B. (2001). *As a gentleman would say.* Nashville, TN: Rutledge Hill Press.

Buggey, T., Toombs, K., Gardener, P., & Cervetti, M. (1999). Training responding behaviors in students with autism: Using videotaped self-modeling. *Journal of Positive Behavioral Interventions, 1,* 205-214.

Buron, K. D. (2003). *When my autism gets too big! A relaxation book for children with autism spectrum disorders.* Shawnee Mission, KS: Autism Asperger Publishing Company.

Buron, K. D., & Curtis, M. (2003). *The incredible 5-point scale: Assisting students with autism spectrum disorders in understanding social interactions and controlling their emotions.* Shawnee Mission, KS: Autism Asperger Publishing Company.

Cardon, T. A. (2004). *Let's talk emotions: Helping children with social cognitive deficits, including AS, HFA, and NVLD, learn to understand and express empathy and emotions.* Shawnee Mission, KS: Autism Asperger Publishing Company.

Carey, T. A., & Bourbon, W. T. (2004). Countercontrol: A new look at some old problems. *Intervention in School and Clinic, 40,* 3-9.

Carothers, D. E., & Taylor, R. L. (2004). Social cognitive processing in elementary school children with Asperger Syndrome. *Education and Training in Developmental Disabilities, 39,* 177-187.

Carr, E. G., Reeve, C. E., & Magito-McLaughlin, D. (1996). Contextual influences on problem behavior in people with developmental disabilities. *Positive behavioral support: Including people with difficult behavior in the community* (pp. 403-423). Baltimore: Paul H. Brookes.

Charlop-Christy, M. H., & Daneshvar, S. (2003). Using video modeling to teach perspective taking to children with autism. *Journal of Positive Behavior Interventions, 5,* 12-21.

Charlop-Christy, M. H., Le, L., & Freeman, K. A. (2000). A comparison of video modeling with in-vivo modeling for teaching children with autism. *Journal of Autism and Developmental Disorders, 30,* 537-552.

Coucouvanis, J. (2005). *Super skills: A social skills group program for children with Asperger Syndrome, high-functioning autism and related challenges.* Shawnee Mission, KS: Autism Asperger Publishing Company.

Cumine, V., Leach, J., & Stevenson, F. (1998). *Asperger Syndrome: A practical guide for teachers.* London: David Fulton.

Dowrick, P. W. (1999). A review of self modeling and related interventions. *Applied and Preventive Psychology, 8,* 23-29.

Dowrick, P. W., & Raeburn, J. M. (1995). Self-modeling: Rapid skills training for children with physical disabilities. *Journal of Developmental and Physical Disabilities, 7,* 25-37

Duke, M. P., Nowicki, S., & Martin, E. A. (1996). *Teaching your child the language of social success.* Atlanta, GA: Peachtree.

Dunn, W., Myles, B. S., & Orr, S. (2002). Sensory processing issues associated with Asperger Syndrome: A preliminary investigation. *The American Journal of Occupational Therapy, 56*(1), 97-102.

Durand, V. M., & Crimmins, D. (1992). *Motivation Assessment Scale.* Topeka, KS: Monaco & Associates.

Espeland, P. (2003). *Life lists for teens.* Minneapolis, MN: Free Spirit Publishing, Inc.

Espin, R. (2003). *Amazingly ... Alphie! Understanding and accepting different ways of being.* Shawnee Mission, KS: Autism Asperger Publishing Company.

Faherty, C. (2000). *What does it mean to me? A workbook explaining self-awareness and life lessons to the child or youth with high functioning autism or Asperger's.* Arlington, TX: Future Horizons.

Frith, U. (1991). *Autism and Asperger Syndrome.* Cambridge: Cambridge University Press.

Gagnon, E., & Myles, B. S. (1999). *This is Asperger Syndrome.* Shawnee Mission, KS: Autism Asperger Publishing Company.

Gagnon, E. (2001). *The Power Card strategy: Using special interests to motivate children and youth with Asperger Syndrome and autism.* Shawnee Mission, KS: Autism Asperger Publishing Company.

Ghaziuddin, M. (2002). Asperger Syndrome: Associated psychiatric and medical conditions. *Focus on Autism and Other Developmental Disabilities, 17,* 138-144.

Gillberg, C. (1993). Autism and related behaviors. *Journal of Intellectual Disability Research, 37,* 343-372.

Goldstein, S., & Schwebach, A. J. (2004). The comorbidity of pervasive developmental disorder and attention deficit hyperactivity disorder: Results of a retrospective chart review. *Journal of Autism and Developmental Disorders, 34,* 329-339.

Grandin, T. (1999, April). *Understanding people with autism: Developing a career makes life satisfying.* Paper presented at the Maap Services, Inc., and Indiana Resource Center for Autism Conference, Indianapolis, IN.

Grandin, T., & Duffy, K. (2004). *Developing talents: Careers for individuals with Asperger Syndrome and high-functioning autism.* Shawnee Mission, KS: Autism Asperger Publishing Company.

Gray, C. (1995). *Social stories unlimited: Social stories and comic strip conversations.* Jenison, MI: Jenison Public Schools.

Gray, C. (2000). *Writing social stories with Carol Gray.* Arlington, TX: Future Horizons.

Gray, C., & Gerand, J. D. (1993). Social stories: Improving responses of students with autism with accurate social information. *Focus on Autistic Behavior, 8,* 1-10.

Gutstein, S. E., & Sheely, R. K. (2002). *Relationship development: Intervention with children, adolescents and adults – Social development activities for Asperger Syndrome, autism PDD and NLD.* London: Jessica Kingsley.

Gutstein, S. E., & Sheely, R. K. (2002). *Relationship development: Intervention with young children – Social and emotional development activities for Asperger's Syndrome, autism PDD and NLD.* London: Jessica Kingsley.

Hadwin, J., Baron-Cohen, S., Howlin, P., & Hill, K. (1996). Can we teach children with autism to understand emotions, belief, or pretence? *Development and Psychopathology, 8,* 345-365.

Howlin, P., Baron-Cohen, S., & Hadwin, J. (1999). *Teaching children with autism to mind-read: A practical guide.* New York: John Wiley & Sons.

Ives, M. (2001). *What is Asperger Syndrome, and how will it affect me? A guide for young people.* Shawnee Mission, KS: Autism Asperger Publishing Company.

Janzen, J. (2003). *Understanding the nature of autism: A guide to autism spectrum disorders* (2nd ed.). San Antonio, TX: Therapy Skill Builders.

Jordan, R., & Powell, S. (1995). *Understanding and teaching children with autism.* New York: John Wiley.

Kahn, J. S., Kehle, T. J., Jenson, W. R., & Clark, E. (1990). Comparison of cognitive-behavioral relaxation, and self-modeling interventions for depression among middle-school students. *School Psychology Review, 19,* 196-211.

Kaland, M., Moller-Nielsen, A., Callsesen, K., Mortensen, E. L., Gottlieb, D., & Smith, L. (2002). A new 'advanced' test of theory of mind: Evidence from children and adolescents with Asperger Syndrome. *Journal of Child Psychology and Psychiatry, 43,* 517-528.

Kamps, D. M., Kravitz, T., & Ross, M. (2002). Social-communicative strategies for school-age children. In H. Goldstein, L. A. Kaczmarek, & K. M. English (Eds.), *Promoting social communication: Children with developmental disabilities from birth to adolescence* (pp. 239-277). Baltimore: Paul H. Brookes.

Kaplan, J. S., & Carter, J. (1995). *Beyond behavior modification: A cognitive-behavioral approach to management in the school* (3rd ed.). Austin, TX: Pro-Ed.

Kauchak, T. (2002). *I can do anything!: Smart cards for strong girls.* Middleton, WI: Pleasant Company Publications.

Kern, L., Dunlap, G., Clarke, S., & Childs, K. (1994). Student-assisted functional assessment interview. *Diagnostique, 19*(2-3), 29-39.

Kerr, M. M., & Nelson, C. M. (1993). *Strategies for managing behavior problems in the classroom.* Columbus, OH: Merrill/Macmillan.

Kozleski, E. B. (1991). Visual symbol acquisition by students with autism. *Exceptionality, 2,* 173-194.

Krantz, P. J., MacDuff, M. T., & McClannahan, L. E. (1993). Programming participation in family activities for children with autism: Parents' use of photographic activity schedules. *Journal of Applied Behavior Analysis, 26,* 89-97.

Kuttler, S., Myles, B. S., & Carlson, J. K. (1998). The use of social stories to reduce precursors to tantrum behavior in a student with autism. *Focus on Autism and Other Developmental Disabilities, 13,* 176-182.

Lawson, J., Baron-Cohen, S., & Wheelwright, S. (2004). Empathising and systemizing in adults with and without Asperger Syndrome. *Journal of Autism and Developmental Disorders, 34,* 301-310.

Ledgin, N. (2002). *Asperger's and self-esteem: Insight and hope through famous role models.* Arlington, TX: Future Horizons.

Leslie, A. M. (1987). Pretense and representation: The origins of a "theory of mind." *Psychological Review, 97,* 122-131.

Lewis, T. J., Scott, T. M., & Sugai, G. (1994). The problem behavior questionnaire: A teacher-based instrument to develop functional hypotheses of problem behavior in general education classrooms. *Diagnostique, 19*(2-3), 103-115.

Long, N. J., Morse, W. C., & Newman, R. G. (1976). *Conflict in the classroom: The educational children with problems* (3rd ed.). Belmont, CA: Wadsworth.

Madden, K. (2002). *Writing smarts: A girl's guide to writing great poetry, stories, school reports, and more!* Middleton, WI: Pleasant Company Publications.

Madison, L. (2002). *The feelings book: The care & keeping of your emotions.* Middleton, WI: Pleasant Company Publications.

McAfee, J. (2002). *Navigating the social world: A curriculum for individuals with Asperger's Syndrome, high functioning autism, and related disorders.* Arlington, TX: Future Horizons.

McConnell, M. E., Hilvitz, P. B., & Cox, C. J. (1998). Functional assessment: A systematic process for assessment and intervention in general and special education classrooms. *Intervention in School and Clinic, 34,* 10-20.

Murdock, L., & Khalsa, G. S. (2003). *Joining in! A program for teaching social skills.* Shawnee Mission, KS: Autism Asperger Publishing Company.

Myles, B. S., Cook, K. T., Miller, N. E., Rinner, L., & Robbins, L. (2000). *Asperger Syndrome and sensory issues: Practical solutions for making sense of the world.* Shawnee Mission, KS: Autism Asperger Publishing Company.

Myles, B. S., Hagiwara, T., Dunn, W., Rinner, L., Reese, M., Huggins, A., & Becker, S. (2004). Sensory issues in children with Asperger Syndrome and autism. *Education and Training in Developmental Disabilities, 3*(4), 283-290.

Myles, B. S., & Simpson, R. L., & Bock, S. (1999). *Asperger Syndrome Diagnostic Scale.* Austin, TX: Pro-Ed.

Myles, B. S., & Simpson, R. L. (2003). *Asperger Syndrome: A guide for educators and parents* (2nd ed.). Austin, TX: Pro-Ed.

Myles, B. S., & Simpson, R. L. (1994a). Prevention and management considerations for aggressive and violent children and youth. *Education and Treatment of Children, 17,* 370-384.

Myles, B. S., & Simpson, R. L. (1994b). Understanding and preventing acts of aggression and violence in school-age children and youth. *Preventing School Failure, 38,* 40-46.

Myles, B. S., & Simpson, R. L. (1998). Aggression and violence by school-age children and youth: Understanding the aggression cycle and prevention/intervention strategies. *Intervention in School and Clinic, 33*, 259-264.

Myles, B. S., & Simpson, R. L. (1999). The aggression cycle and teacher strategies for prevention/intervention. *The Prevention Researcher, 6*(2), 9-11.

Myles, B. S., & Simpson, R. L. (2003). *Asperger Syndrome: A guide for educators and parents.* Austin, TX: Pro-Ed.

Myles, B. S., Trautman, M. L., & Schelvan, R. L. (2004). *The hidden curriculum: Practical solutions for understanding unstated rules in social situations.* Shawnee Mission, KS: Autism Asperger Publishing Company.

O'Neill, R. E., Horner, R. H., Albin, R. W., Sprague, J. R., Storey, K., & Newton, J. S. (1997). *Functional assessment and program development for problem behavior: A practical handbook* (2nd ed.). Albany, NY: Brooks/Cole.

Packer, A. J. (1992). *Bringing up parents: The teenager's handbook.* Minneapolis, MN: Free Spirit Publishing.

Packer, A. J. (1997). *How rude! The teenager's guide to good manners, proper behavior, and not grossing people out.* Minneapolis, MN: Free Spirit Publishing.

Powers, M. D. (2000). *Children with autism: A parents' guide* (2nd ed.). Bethesda, MD: Woodbine House.

Powers, M. (2003). *Children with autism: A parents' guide.* Bethesda, MD: Woodbine House.

Powers, M. D. (2003). *Asperger Syndrome and your child: A parents' guide.* Bethesda, MD: Woodbine House.

Quill, K. A. (1995). *Teaching children with autism: Strategies to enhance communication and socialization.* New York: Delmar Publishers.

Raymer, D. (2002). *Staying home alone: A girl's guide to feeling safe and having fun.* Middleton, WI: Pleasant Company Publications.

Rogers, M. F., & Myles, B. S. (2001). Using social stories and comic strip conversations to interpret social situations for an adolescent with Asperger Syndrome. *Intervention in School and Clinic, 36*, 310-313.

Schaefer, V. L. (1998). *The care & keeping of you: The body book for girls.* Middleton, WI: Pleasant Company Publications.

Simblett, G. J., & Wilson, D. N. (1993). Asperger's Syndrome: Three cases and a discussion. *Journal of Intellectual Disability Research, 37*, 85-97

Spivack, G., Platt, J. J., & Shure, M. (1976). *The problem-solving approach to adjustment.* San Francisco: Jossey-Bass.

Swaggart, B., Gagnon, E., Bock, S., Earles, T., Quinn, C., Myles, B. S., & Simpson, R. (1995). Using social stories to teach social and behavioral skills to children with autism. *Focus on Autistic Behavior, 10*, 1-16.

Tiger, C. (2003). *How to behave: A guide to modern manners for the socially challenged.* Philadelphia, PA: Quirk Books.

University of Cambridge. (2003). *Mind reading.* Cambridge, England: Author.

Valentine, M. R. (1987). *How to deal with discipline problems in the schools: A practical guide for educators.* Dubuque, IA: Kendall Hunt.

Williams, M. S., & Shellenberger, S. (1996). *How does your engine run: A leader's guide to the alert program for self-regulation.* Albuquerque, NM: TherapyWorks, Inc.

Williams, K. (1995). Understanding the student with Asperger Syndrome: Guidelines for teachers. *Focus on Autistic Behavior, 10*(2), 9-16.

Williams, K. (2001). Understanding the student with Asperger Syndrome: Guidelines for teachers. *Intervention in School and Clinic, 36,* 287-292.

Wing, L. (1981). Asperger's Syndrome: A clinical account. *Psychological Medicine, 11,* 115-129.

Winner, M. G. (2000). *Inside out: What makes a person with social cognitive deficits tick?* San Jose, CA: Author.

Winner, M. G. (2002). *Thinking about you, thinking about me: Philosophy and strategies to further develop perspective taking and communicative abilities for persons with social cognitive deficits.* San Jose, CA: Author.

Wolfberg, P. J. (2003). *Peer play and the autism spectrum: The art of guiding children's socialization and imagination.* Shawnee Mission, KS: Autism Asperger Publishing Company.

World Health Organization. (1992). *International classification of diseases and related health problems* (10th ed.). Geneva: Author.

Index

Read AAPC's Entire Practical Solutions Series

**Asperger Syndrome and Difficult Moments:
Practical Solutions for Tantrums, Rage,
and Meltdowns – *Revised and Expanded Edition***
Brenda Smith Myles and Jack Southwick

**Asperger Syndrome and Adolescence:
Practical Solutions for School Success**
Brenda Smith Myles and Diane Adreon

**Asperger Syndrome and the Elementary School
Experience: Practical Solutions for Academic &
Social Difficulties**
Susan Thompson Moore

**Asperger Syndrome and Sensory Issues:
Practical Solutions for Making Sense
of the World**
*Brenda Smith Myles, Katherine Tapscott
Cook, Nancy E. Miller, Louann Rinner and
Lisa A. Robbins*

**The Hidden Curriculum: Practical Solutions for
Understanding Unstated Rules in Social
Situations**
*Brenda Smith Myles, Melissa L. Trautman,
and Ronda L. Schelvan; foreword by Michelle
Garcia Winner*

**Perfect Targets: Asperger Syndrome and
Bullying; Practical Solutions for
Surviving the Social World**
Rebekah Heinrichs

**Practical Solutions to Everyday Challenges for
Children with Asperger Syndrome**
Haley Morgan Myles

NEW!

Difficult Moments for Children and Youth with Autism Spectrum Disorders
DVD; playing time: 25 minutes
Brenda Smith Myles

The Hidden Curriculum: Teaching What Is Meaningful
DVD; playing time: 46:30 minutes
Brenda Smith Myles

A**P**C Autism Asperger Publishing Company

To order, call **913-897-1004**, fax to **913-681-9473**
visit our website at **www.asperger.net** or mail to **AAPC • P.O. Box 23173 Shawnee Mission, KS 66283-0173**

- -

NAME

ADDRESS

CITY   STATE   ZIP

PHONE   EMAIL

CODE	TITLE	PRICE	QTY.	TOTAL
9901a	Asperger Syndrome and Difficult Moments	$21.95		
9908	Asperger Syndrome and Adolescence	$23.95		
9911	Asperger Syndrome and the Elementary School Experience	$23.95		
9907a	Asperger Syndrome and Sensory Issues	$21.95		
9942	The Hidden Curriculum: Practical Solutions	$19.95		
9918	Perfect Targets: Asperger Syndrome and Bullying	$21.95		
9917	Practical Solutions to Everyday Challenges	$12.95		
	PRACTICAL SOLUTION SERIES (ALL SEVEN BOOKS IN SERIES)	$126.00		
9721	The Hidden Curriculum: Teaching What Is Meaningful (DVD)	$44.95		
9720	Difficult Moments for Children and Youth (DVD)	$44.95		

SHIPPING AND HANDLING/USA

Order Total	Ground
$1 – $50	$5
$51 – $100	$8
$101 – $200	$10
$201 – $300	$20
$301 – $400	$30
Over $400	10% of subtotal

For rush, international or Canadian deliveries,
please call toll-free 1-877-277-8254.

SUBTOTAL $ _____

7.5% KS SALES TAX   + _____
(Kansas Residents Only)

SHIPPING & HANDLING   + _____

TOTAL   _____

METHOD OF PAYMENT

☐ AMEX   ☐ VISA   ☐ DISCOVER   ☐ MASTERCARD   ☐ P.O. ATTACHED
☐ CHECK/MONEY ORDER ENCLOSED (PAYABLE TO AAPC)

ACCOUNT #

☐☐☐☐☐☐☐☐☐☐☐☐☐☐☐☐☐☐☐

EXP. DATE ☐☐ — ☐☐   SIGNATURE _____
(Required to process your order)